H. B. CHARLES JR.

D1259958

It Happens After Prayer

Biblical Motivation for Believing Prayer

MOODY PUBLISHERS

CHICAGO

All Scripture quotations, unless otherwise indicated, are taken from
The Holy Bible, English Standard Version. Copyright © 2000; 2001 by
Crossway Bibles, a division of Good News Publishers.

Scripture quotations marked NIV are taken from the *Holy Bible, New
International Version*®, NIV®. Copyright © 1973, 1978, 1984 by Biblica,
Inc.™ Used by permission of Zondervan. All rights reserved worldwide.
www.zondervan.com

Scripture quotations marked NKJV are taken from the *New King James
Version*. Copyright © 1982 by Thomas Nelson, Inc. Used by permission.
All rights reserved.

Edited by Jim Vincent
Interior and Cover design: Smartt Guys design
Cover image: Wavebreak Media / 123RF
Author Photo: Derrick Wilson

Library of Congress Cataloging-in-Publication Data
Charles, H. B.
  It happens after prayer : Biblical motivation for believing prayer /
H.B. Charles, Jr.
    pages cm
  Includes bibliographical references and index.
  ISBN 978-0-8024-0725-2 (alk. paper)
  1. Prayer—Christianity. I. Title.
  BV210.3.C43 2013
  248.3'2—dc23

                                                    2013002309

We hope you enjoy this book from Moody Publishers. Our goal is to provide high-quality, thought-provoking books and products that connect
truth to your real needs and challenges. For more information on other
books and products written and produced from a biblical perspective, go
to www.moodypublishers.com or write to:

Moody Publishers
820 N. LaSalle Boulevard
Chicago, IL 60610

3 5 7 9 10 8 6 4 2

Printed in the United States of America

Praise for *It Happens After Prayer*

Reading *It Happens After Prayer* is like plugging your prayer life into an electrical socket. You will walk away motivated and inspired by the truths of Scripture about the centrality of our prayer lives.

> —BRYAN CARTER
> Senior Pastor, Concord Church, Dallas

Pastor Charles is a man of prayer. This and his knowledge of God's Word shine through this book. He is faithful to the text as well as practical in his presentation. If you want to apply such knowledge to your personal life, this book is for you. H.B.'s work will be an extreme help.

> —GEORGE E. HURTT
> Senior Pastor, Mt. Sinai Baptist Church, Los Angeles

In a day when people have reduced prayer to skillful negotiation and a means of manipulating the will of God, Pastor Charles makes it clear that prayer is mysteriously simple—and that for this contemporary generation we can set up a cyberspace cafe and a chat room with God anywhere.

> —MELVIN V. WADE SR., Senior Pastor,
> Mt. Moriah Baptist Church, Los Angeles

In *It Happens After Prayer*, H. B. Charles encourages all Christians to pray with the confident belief that God hears and answers prayer. Read this book, and your prayer life won't be the same! Pastor Charles is not only one of the powerful preachers of his generation, but he has proven to be equally persuasive with pen in hand. He writes with both a commitment to biblical accuracy and the loving heart of an experienced pastor.

> —MAURICE WATSON, Senior Pastor,
> Beulahland Bible Church, Macon, Georgia

In a world where preachers and teachers promote a God who can be likened unto an ecclesiastical bellhop, a theological redcap, a Christological Santa Claus, and a Trinitarian vending machine, it is refreshing, renewing, and reinvigorating to read a biblically saturated and theologically based book from the hands of an astute expositor, Dr. H. B. Charles. This book provides both the biblical methodology for praying and furnishes the assurance from God's Word that the pray-ers need not *pry* the door open, rather they can *pray* the door open. This work whets the appetite for prayer and prepares the heart for the assurance that will come when believers know the will of God because they have become intimately acquainted with the God of the will.

> —DR. ROBERT SMITH JR., Professor of Divinity Christian Preaching, Beeson Divinity School

If you are like me, you've thought about prayer, talked about prayer, and encouraged others to pray . . . more than you've actually prayed. H.B. has helped us in this book return to prayer as intimate relationship with God. How refreshing! May you find in these pages motivation to close your door, fall on your face, and talk with the God of heaven and earth. Thanks, H.B.!

> —CHARLIE DATES, Senior Pastor, Progressive Baptist Church, Chicago

To my father,
H. B. Charles Sr.

Contents

Foreword

I first met H. B. Charles Jr. through the Internet.

I had written a brief note on my weblog about a well-known preacher who was, in my estimation, a true pastoral expositor. I made the comment more or less in passing and didn't even stop to define it. A few days later I received a note from a young pastor in Los Angeles asking me to explain what I meant. Little did I know that that simple query would lead to an enduring friendship.

For many years H. B. (which is how his friends refer to him) pastored the church in Los Angeles that his father had pastored. Following your own father into the same pulpit would be quite a challenge for anyone. He mentions in this book how that challenge shaped him and taught him to depend upon the Lord.

A few years ago H. B. accepted the call to move across the country to pastor a large congregation in Jacksonville, Florida. By God's grace, my friend has proved to be more than equal to the task. I have seen with my own eyes the great work being done at Shiloh Metropolitan Baptist Church. Under his guidance, the church has grown numerically, spiritually and in influence locally and across the nation.

Not long ago I had the chance to sit under his ministry for three days. What a feast we enjoyed as he opened the Word of God with clarity, passion, and much spiritual power.

How it is that a young man (he is not yet forty) not only pastors a large congregation but preaches in some of the largest churches in America with evident blessing along the way? I cannot explain it all, but I know this much. H.B. Charles Jr. is a man of prayer. He knows how to pray, he knows the power of prayer, and he believes that when God is taken at His Word, we may pray and see great things happen in our day.

To that end he has written this wonderful book called *It Happens After Prayer*. As I read it, I thought to myself that it is easy for preachers to make people feel guilty about prayer. We can always pray more. We know that. We ought to pray more. We know that too. Who among us would dare to say that we are masters of prayer?

Because H.B. knows this, he writes not to increase our guilt but to encourage us to pray. God wants us to pray; He has opened the very door of heaven and said, "Bring your petitions and come right in. I want to hear from you."

I can't think of a higher compliment than to say that a book on prayer made me want to pray.

I hope that happens to you too. If your prayer life feels anemic, read this book and let God's truth fill your heart and give you strength.

RAY PRITCHARD
President, Keep Believing Ministries
Author of *An Anchor for the Soul, Stealth Attack*

It Happens After
Prayer

*Call to me and I will answer you, and will tell you great
and hidden things that you have not known.*

JEREMIAH 33:3

Life happens. Faith weakens. Temptations attack. Satan oppresses. Needs overwhelm. Sickness comes. Finances disappear. Divorce looms. Loneliness suffocates. Friends betray. In addition, decisions paralyze. Worries strangle. Careers stall.

The challenges of life confront us all. You cannot cancel your appointment with trouble. And you do not know when pain will show up in your life. Just be sure it's coming. There is nothing you can do to stop it.

That's the bad news. Here is the good news: Though you may not be able to control what happens to you in life, you can control how you respond. This is the wonderful benefit of the Christian life. To trust in Jesus Christ as your Savior and Lord does not bring an end to all of your troubles, no matter what some high-profile religious personalities falsely teach. To the contrary, following Christ will produce trials that you would never face otherwise (John 16:33; Acts 14:22; 2 Timothy 3:12). Christianity is a battleground, not a playground. But faith in God ensures that you will never have to stand and fight alone (Ephesians 6:10–20). The believer can live with the assurance that the Lord is there (Psalm 46:1).

Yes, Christianity is a battleground. Yet *the presence of your divine Ally provides sufficient resources for every struggle you face*.

I repeat. There is nothing you can do to stop bad things from happening in your life. But you can determine your response.

You can turn the other cheek.

You can go the second mile.

You can love those who hate you.

You can bless those who persecute you.

You can forgive those who offend you seven times in one day.

You can overcome evil with good.

You can be steadfast, immovable, and always abounding in the work of the Lord.

You can give thanks in all circumstances.

You can count it all joy when you meet trials of various kinds.[1]

In his little book, *Wishful Thinking*, Frederick Buechner defines what a Christian is for the uninitiated. "A Christian isn't necessarily any nicer than anybody else," he concludes. "Just better informed."[2] Isn't that wonderful? Being a Christian does not make me superior to the unbelievers around me. It does give me options that the unbeliever does not have, or even know are available. Therefore, I do not have to respond to my problems as those who do not know God. I can choose to be happy. I can choose to trust. I can choose to love. I can choose to forgive. I can choose to hope again.

Some people are like thermometers. They only register the condition of their surroundings. Other people are like thermostats. They regulate the conditions they find themselves in. Their circumstances do not dictate how they think or feel or act. They have a spiritual "climate control" that enables them to be strong and stable and steadfast, whatever the situation.

The apostle Paul wrote to his friends in Philippi, "I know how to be brought low, and I know how to abound. In any and every circumstance, I have learned the secret of facing plenty and hunger, abundance and need. I can do all things through him who strengthens me" (Philippians 4:12–13). That is the testimony of a thermostat.

How do you respond to life's dangers, toils, and snares? Are you a thermometer or a thermostat? What do you do when life tumbles in on you? Do you try to manage the overwhelming circumstances of life with your own strength, wisdom, and resources? To try is to be like the young man who just received his plumber's license. A friend took him to see the Niagara Falls. He stared intently at it for several minutes, and then whispered, "I think I can fix this." No, you can't.

Or do you endeavor to manage your pain and problems with work, money, toys, alcohol, drugs, entertainment, pleasure, or the myriad of other vanities the world offers? This won't work either. John wisely warns,

> Do not love the world or the things in the world. If anyone loves the world, the love of the Father is not in him. For all that is in the world—the desires of the flesh and the desires of the eyes and pride of life—is not from the Father but is from the world. And the world is passing away along with its desires, but whoever does the will of God abides forever. (1 John 2:15–17)

There is only one reliable option for responding to the things that you would change if you could, but you've tried and you cannot. It is what Moses did when the burden of leading the children of Israel got the best of him. It is what King Jehoshaphat did when he did not know what to do about the coalition of nations that were planning to attack God's people. It is what Nehemiah did when he received the bad news about the broken down walls of Jerusalem. It is what David did as he hid in a cave to escape Saul who sought to take his life. It is what Daniel did before an open window, even though he knew it would land him in a lions' den. It is what the church did at Mary's house, the night before Peter was to be put to death by Herod. It is what Paul and Silas did in the middle of the night, as they sat in jail on trumped-up charges. It is what Jesus Himself did in the garden of Gethsemane, as He agonized in the shadow of the cross.

You ought to pray about these things.

WHY PRAY?

Why pray? Will God hear our prayers? Does He care? Does prayer really make a difference? What can we realistically expect from God when we pray?

There are many good and important reasons why you should pray. In fact, it would be of great benefit for you to study the Scriptures to find out what they teach about why you should pray. But that is not the focus of this book. This is not a textbook that explains the whys and hows of prayer. My goal is to simply challenge you to respond to the vicissitudes of life with prayer, to pray without ceasing, and to pray with great expectations. To that end, let me highlight just the two most essential reasons you should pray.

GOD COMMANDS WE PRAY

You should pray because the Word of God commands you to pray. This should be all the reasoning we need to govern our attitude and actions toward prayer. As Christians, our chief concern in determining how we should view a subject is to answer this question: "What does the Word of God say about it?" If you are like me, you have a long way to go in submitting every area of your life to the authority of Christ. But our attitude must be there before our actions can catch up.

As a teenager, I was given a bumper sticker that reads: "If it's God's will, I will." I still have it in my study to constantly remind me that He deserves and demands my total allegiance, unconditional surrender, and complete obedience. This is why I am committed to be steadfast in prayer, even though my flesh constantly struggles against it. Prayer is an act of obedience to God. Even if there were no practical benefits to prayer (and there are many), we should be devoted to prayer simply because the Word of God commands it.

Prayer expresses our submission to and dependence upon God. The things you pray about are the things you trust God to handle.

Scripture does not present prayer as an optional response to life's challenges. Prayer is a divine mandate. The prophet exhorted, "Seek the Lord while he may be found; call upon him while he is near" (Isaiah 55:6). "Call to me and I will answer you," says the Lord, "and will tell you great and hidden things that you have not known" (Jeremiah 33:3). In the Sermon on the Mount, the Lord Jesus declared, "Ask, and it will be given to you; seek, and you will find; knock, and it will be opened to you" (Matthew 7:7). The apostle Paul instructs, "Do not be anxious about anything, but in everything by prayer and supplication with thanksgiving let your requests be made known to God" (Philippians 4:6). James asked, "Is anyone . . . suffering?" Then he advised, "Let him pray" (James 5:13).

Prayer is our Christian duty. It is an expression of submission to God and dependence upon Him. For that matter, prayer is arguably the most objective measurement of our dependence upon God. Think of it this way. The things you pray about are the things you trust God to handle. The things you neglect to pray about are the things you trust you can handle on your own.

Can you see why God commands us to pray? Prayer reflects our confidence in the heavenly Father to care for our needs. When my kids ask me for something, I typically respond by reminding them their dad is a "poor black preacher." But this does not discourage them in the least, even when they are asking for something I really can't afford. Their confidence in their father's ability to provide for them brings me so much joy. Moreover, God the Father delights in His children bringing their needs and wants to Him in prayer. It brings glory to the Father to respond to His children who pray in faith. But it grieves the Father when we take our problems to others but refuse to pray.

Believing prayer is our sacred duty to the heavenly Father. "Continuing steadfast in prayer," instructs Paul, "being watchful in it with thanksgiving" (Colossians 4:2). What does it mean to "continue steadfastly in prayer"? It means to be devoted, fervent, and persistent in prayer. Let me bottom-line that for you: Don't stop praying!

Be constant in prayer. Do whatever it takes to maintain and sustain your prayer life. Keep your heart in a posture of prayer before God. Pray for the will of God by praying according to the Word of God. Set a time every day for prayer and Scripture intake. Establish a personal prayer list. Develop friendships with other believers with whom you can partner in prayer. Pray when you feel like it. Pray when you don't feel like it. Pray until you feel like it. Ruth Bell Graham said it well: "Pray when you feel like it, for it is a sin to neglect such an opportunity. Pray when you don't feel like it, for it is dangerous to remain in such a condition."

The words of the beloved hymn "What a Friend We Have in

Jesus" have become a part of my personal theology. I know they are just words of a song, not the divine revelation of Scripture. But they are true, nonetheless.

> What a Friend we have in Jesus, all our sins and griefs to bear!
> What a privilege to carry everything to God in prayer!
> O what peace we often forfeit, O what needless pain we bear,
> All because we do not carry everything to God in prayer.[3]

I have lived long enough to know and accept the fact that some pain is necessary, inevitable, and even beneficial. I fully accept this reality. But I have determined that I do not want to experience any needless pains. If I do not *have* to experience it, I don't want to. Yet the truth is that we have all suffered unnecessarily, because we did not take everything to God in prayer.

Before you read another paragraph, pause and simply renew your commitment to the duty of prayer. Ask the Lord to help you continue steadfastly in prayer.

PRAYER IS A PRIVILEGE

After obedience to the Word of God, there is another essential reason you should be devoted to prayer. This second reason for the praying life is what the rest of this book is about. I hope you will read to the end. But here's the point right up front. I can't resist; this news is almost too good to be true. Better yet, it's too good not to be true: Only a good and wise and sovereign God like ours would make prayer a duty and a privilege at the same time.

Let me say that again. Prayer is a privilege. It is not a burdensome duty. It is a wonderful privilege. Even though Scripture commands us to pray, we should not view prayer as something we *have* to do. We should view is as something we *get* to do.

It is a privilege to have an audience before the Creator and Sustainer of the universe. The blood and righteousness of the Lord Jesus Christ has given us access to the throne of grace. Every redeemed follower of Christ is granted an open door before the Lord Almighty. We can approach God in prayer with confidence. There we can obtain the grace and mercy we need (see Hebrews 4:16).

Yet the privilege of prayer is greater still. Not only does God command us to bring our needs to Him; He also promises to hear and answer our prayers.

"Why should I pray?" you ask. Answer: Prayer works! More accurately, God works when we pray. When we work, we work. When we pray, God works. Charles Spurgeon said, "Prayer is the slender nerve that moves the arm of omnipotence."

> **We should not view prayer as something we *have* to do but as something we *get* to do.**

In Ephesians 3:14–19, Paul makes some incredible requests on the behalf of the saints. In a prayer for spiritual enablement, he asks that the saints would be able to "know the love of Christ that surpasses knowledge" (v. 19).

Come again? How can you know something that is beyond knowledge? That's incredible. However, Paul's remarkable prayer requests begin to make sense when you read the doxology in the next verse: "Now to him who is able to do far more abundantly than all that we ask or think, according to the power at work within us" (v. 20). This truth applies to every prayer you pray. God is more than able to answer your prayers. What a promise! Whatever you are thinking about or asking for, God is able to do far more than that for you.

Whatever you are thinking about or asking for, God is able to do far more than that for you.

Do not misunderstand me. You should not view prayer as some rigged slot machine that gives you a jackpot every time you make a request. This book is not advocating "prosperity theology." I am not claiming that you can write your own ticket with God by faith. Prayer does not guarantee your life will be an unbroken cycle of health, wealth, success, and happiness. Prayer doesn't work that way.

GOD ANSWERS PRAYERS ACCORDING TO HIS WILL

I believe in the exhaustive sovereignty of God, which is just a fancy way of saying that God is God. That is, God is God alone. This means that our prayers do not put God under obligation to do whatever we ask. It does not matter how long you pray. It does not matter how loud you cry. It does not matter how many verses you quote or promises you claim. It does not matter how many so-called positive confessions you make. As you pray, you must remember who God is. You must also remember where God is. Our God is in heaven, doing whatever pleases Him (Psalm 103:19). This is the basis upon which God answers prayer. God works all things according to the counsel of His will (Ephesians 1:11).

I had a head-on collision with this reality when I was sixteen years old. I was invited to Detroit to preach a weeklong youth revival. This was a big deal. I had never been that far away from home for that long to preach. I was beyond excited. But when it was time to leave, I had mixed emotions. My father was in the hospital. It was the first time in my life my father had ever been admitted to the hospital. He would be in the hospital the entire week. He was scheduled to come home the day I would return from Detroit.

A week later, as I was flying back to home to Los Angeles—to my father and family—my dad died. My brother and a friend waited for me at the airport; they too were unaware of his passing. They had been instructed to rush me to the hospital to see my dad, hoping to get me there before it was too late. When we arrived and asked for my father's room, I was told someone would come out to speak with me. Before they could come, I was being rushed home. Still no one told me what was going on. But I sensed something was terribly wrong.

During that ride home, I prayed harder than I have ever prayed about anything in my life. I quickly came to grips with the fact that it was my father's last day in this world. Yet I had what I thought to be a simple request. "Lord, please let me say goodbye to my father." With everything that was in me, I pleaded with the Lord to give me the opportunity to give my love to my dad before he was taken away from me. But when we pulled into the driveway, a family friend was there to break the news to me.

This was the most fervent prayer I had ever prayed. And the answer was no. But I write the next sentence without any hesitation, reservation, or qualification. God answers prayer. Today I am several decades removed from my father's death. And in the intervening years, God has done far more for me than I could ask or think. As I look at that experience in the rearview mirror of life, I thank God that He did not give me what I desperately requested that day. Before that experience, I believed prayer changes things. After that experience, I learned that prayer changes me. My life and relationship with the Lord were never the same since that day the Lord told me no. I am convinced that prayer works, even when it does not work the way you want it to work.

> **Looking through the rearview mirror of life, I thank God that He did not give me what I desperately requested that day.**

This is what the apostle Paul learned when he was "given a thorn in [the] flesh" (2 Corinthians 12:7 NIV). We do not know what this thorn was. But the language conveys the fact that it hurt. Paul responded with prayer. He asked the Lord three times to remove the thorn in the flesh. The Lord refused to do so. He did not give Paul what he asked. But He gave him something better. "My grace is sufficient for you," said the Lord, "for my power is made perfect in weakness." This transformed Paul's perspective. He concluded, "Therefore I will boast all the more gladly of my weaknesses, so that the power of Christ may rest upon me. For the sake of Christ, then, I am content with weaknesses, insults, hardships, persecutions, and calamities. For when I am weak, then I am strong" (2 Corinthians 12:9–10).

This can be your experience, too. It happens after prayer! What happens after prayer? I'm glad you asked. "It" is a fill-in-the-blank that you can complete with any issue in your life. Whatever that special thing is that you need the Lord to do in your life, it happens after prayer.

Do you need faith to see beyond your circumstances?

Do you need divine intervention for a difficult situation?

Do you need relief from pain, grief, or sorrow?

Do you need strength to resist a temptation?

Do you need victory over some besetting sin in your life?

Do you need wisdom for a tough decision you have to make?

Do you need a door of opportunity opened for you?

Do you need healing or restoration of health?

Do you need reconciliation in some broken relationship?

Do you need grace to be faithful in a hard assignment?

Do you need assurance that God is on your side?

Each one of these happens after prayer! There are a lot of things you can do to fix your situation after you pray. But there is nothing you can do to fix the situation until you pray. Whatever it is you need God to do in your life, it happens after prayer.

A father and his son were riding their bikes together one day. As they rode down the trail, the father eyed a large branch that had fallen in the path ahead. Instead of riding around it, the father decided to use this as an opportunity to teach his son an important lesson. They pulled over, and the father instructed his son to move the branch out of the way.

The boy pushed and pulled, but was unable to move the branch. "I can't do it," he said, exhausted. "Sure you can, Son," replied the father. "Be sure to use all your strength." The boy tried harder. But he could not move the branch.

Near tears, he said again, "I can't do it."

"Did you use all of your strength?" The father asked.

"Yes," the boy answered.

"No you didn't," the father replied. "You didn't ask me to help you."

What is the obstacle in your path? What is it in your life that you have tried to move without success? Have you used all of your strength? No you haven't—if you have not asked God's help and prayed about it sincerely, diligently, and persistently.

It happens after prayer.

CHAPTER 2

God Is Not a
Sleepy Friend

*I tell you, though he will not get up and give him anything
because he is his friend, yet because of his impudence
he will rise and give him whatever he needs.*

LUKE 11:8

The disciples watched and waited as Jesus prayed. When He finished talking to the Father, one of the disciples had a question. Speaking for the rest, he said, "Lord, John the Baptist taught his disciples how to pray. Would you teach us how to pray?" (see Luke 11:1). This nameless disciple's request prompted the lesson on prayer (Luke 11:2–13). In this chapter, I want to focus your attention on the Jesus' instructions. But let's consider the disciples' request first.

When was this request made? The disciples asked Jesus to teach them how to pray after observing Him in prayer. This was not the first time they had seen Jesus pray. The references to the prayer life of Jesus in Luke's Gospel alone make it clear that Jesus was devoted to prayer (see Luke 3:21; 6:12; 9:28–29; 22:31–32, 39–46). The regular, passionate, and reverent times of prayer that Jesus practiced moved and motivated the disciples. Finally, they asked Jesus to teach them to have the same sense of personal communion with God the Father. In this, the disciples should be our example. One of the primary reasons why you and I ought to pray is because Jesus prayed. Think about it. Jesus is the God-Man, the blending of complete deity and perfect humanity. In Him the whole fullness of deity dwells bodily (Colossians 2:9). Yet Jesus prayed. And if Jesus felt it necessary to pray, how much more do we need to learn how pray.

To whom was this request made? The disciples asked Jesus to teach them to pray. This obvious point is significant. If you want to develop a new skill, learn a new trade, or nurture a new discipline, wisdom will lead you to consult a qualified expert to teach or train you. That's what the disciples did. Who can better teach you how to pray than the Lord Jesus? Being fully human, Jesus knows all about offering prayer. Being fully divine, Jesus knows all about answering prayer. Do you really want to learn how to pray? Go to the feet of Jesus and ask, "Lord, teach us to pray."

Why is this request so important? Luke 11:1 is the only place in the Gospels where the disciples directly ask Jesus to teach them something. They asked Jesus to teach them how to pray, not to preach or do miracles. In Luke 9 and 10, Jesus sent out the disciples with power to preach and perform miracles. When they returned, they reported that even demons were subject to them in Christ's name (Luke 10:17). Yet they still needed to learn how to pray. Why? I believe the wonder-working disciples made this request because prayer is one of the most difficult things to learn as a follower of Christ. Harder than preaching and doing miracles! It is one of the hardest lessons to learn because it is one of the most important things to learn in your Christian life. No wonder the disciples asked, "Lord, teach us how to pray, as John taught his disciples."

> **Prayer is one of the most difficult things to learn as a follower of Christ . . . because it is one of the most important things to learn in your Christian life.**

There is no biblical record of John the Baptist in prayer or teaching his disciples to pray. But this passing statement by the disciples of Jesus is sufficient to conclude that Jesus did teach them. It was customary for rabbis to teach their disciples how to pray. A rabbi would teach his disciples his theory and manner of prayer. This seems to be what the disciples of Jesus expected from Him. They assumed Jesus would teach them His formula for prayer. The "Jesus secret" way to pray. It was the right request. But it was the wrong perspective. They were thinking about the form of prayer, when they should have focused on the object of prayer—God the Father.

Jesus granted their request in an unexpected way. He answered the question they should have been asking. Instead of teaching them a technique, He taught them a truth. Here it is: God answers prayer. This is the most important lesson you can learn about prayer. There is no more encouraging motivation to pray. Prayer matters because it works. Better yet, God works when we pray. God is willing and able to answer prayer. It pleases Him when we pray. The Father delights to hear and answer the prayers of His children. Prayer is the Lord's appointed means to give us what we need from Him.

How then should we pray?

PRAY WITH REVERENCE FOR GOD

Luke 11:2–4 records what is commonly called "The Lord's Prayer." But this is not a prayer that Jesus could have prayed. He never committed any sin that would require Him to ask for forgiveness (verse 4). And praise God for that! You cannot be a sinner and a Savior at the same time. This is our problem. This is why we need a Savior. This is why God sent His only Son to die for our sins on the cross. Christ is qualified to save sinners because He was not one.

So it may be more appropriate to call this "The Model Prayer." It closely parallels the famous prayer recorded in Matthew 6:9–13. But Luke's record is a direct response to the disciples' request that Jesus teach them how to pray. Here Jesus teaches an essential principle for effective prayer: The God who answers prayer is God. Did you get that? God is not the man upstairs. God is not some cosmic ATM machine. God is not a heavenly Santa Claus. God is not a winning lottery ticket.

God is God. God alone is absolutely sovereign, infinitely wise, and unchanging in His goodness. God is wonderful, perfect, awesome, terrible, and majestic in every way. So we must not allow our access to God through Christ to lead us to take His greatness for granted. We must pray God-sized, God-centered, God-exalting prayers.

What does it mean to pray with reverence?

Pray directly to God. Jesus said, "When you pray, say: 'Father.'" (Luke 11:2). Older translations read, "Our Father in heaven," carrying over the words of Matthew 6:9. But in the Greek text, Jesus simply teaches the disciples to address God as "Father." "Our Father in heaven" affirms both the transcendence and immanence of God. But the one word address—"Father"—emphasizes God's closeness, immanence, and nearness.

We should find it difficult to get past this opening address—Father. We should linger there. We should rejoice in it. We should stand in awe of God's gracious condescension. We have the privilege of bringing our needs and wants and sins and hurts and fears directly to God in prayer. Not a priest or patron saint or guardian angel. God. And we do not have to approach God like some desperate beggar asking a rich stranger for a big favor. We can go to God as little children going to a caring father.

> **"Our Father in heaven" affirms both the transcendence and immanence of God. Stand in awe of God's gracious condescension.**

In the Old Testament, the children of Israel had many different names for God. But they rarely addressed God as "Father," and never in a personal, individual sense. But when Jesus taught His disciples how to approach God in prayer, He did not give them a list of Old Testament names to memorize. He taught them to address God directly as our Father.

Jesus can authorize us to pray this way because He is our great High Priest, who makes intimate communion with God possible. We are beneficiaries of God's open-door policy because of Jesus Christ:

> Since then we have a great high priest who has passed through the heavens, Jesus, the Son of God, let us hold fast our confession. For we do not have a high priest who is unable to sympathize with our weaknesses, but one who in every respect has been tempted as we are, yet without sin. Let us then with confidence draw near to the throne of grace, that we may receive mercy and find grace to help in time of need. (Hebrews 4:14–16)

Pray about things that will bring glory to God. In the opening petitions of His prayer (Luke 11:2–3), Jesus rebukes the prayers that rush into God's presence with a grocery list of personal requests. God's name, God's kingdom, and God's will should be our top priorities in prayer. Prayer is about God accomplishing His will on earth, not about you accomplishing your will in heaven. The ultimate purpose of prayer is God and His glory, not you and your needs. Prayer is not about prayer itself. It is not about the answers you may get to your prayers. And it's definitely not about you. It is about God. True prayer is God-centered.

James warns, "You ask and do not receive, because you ask wrongly, to spend it on your passions" (James 4:3). Selfish prayer dishonors God. Prayer works when you pray about things that bring glory to God. Pray that God's name would be hallowed. Pray that God's kingdom comes. Pray that the will of God is done on earth as it is in heaven.

Imagine a father playing with his small children. He sits on the couch with several coins in his hand. His children sit on his lap and work to get his fingers open. One by one, they pry his fingers open. Then they snatch the coins and happily run away. The father is left sitting alone. Is this how you pray? Do you only come to the Father for the coins in His hand? Are your health, finances, family, career, and goals your consuming focus in prayer? Indeed, God is able to work mightily on your behalf in these personal matters. God is gracious and willing to act on your behalf. But don't get fixated with the pennies in His hands. Seek the face of God, not His hand.

Instead of wrestling for coins in the Father's hands, go after the really big stuff. "You make known to me the path of life," David sings. "In your presence there is fullness of joy; at your right hand are pleasures forevermore" (Psalm 16:11).

Pray as if everything depends on God. Jesus rebukes the kind of prayer that rushes into God's presence with a grocery list of personal requests. But that does not mean your personal requests do not matter to God. They matter. God wants you to bring them to Him in prayer. The later petitions of the Model Prayer teach us to pray personally. You can pray about your personal needs: "Give us each day our daily bread" (Luke 11:3). You can pray about your past sins: "and forgive us our sins, for we ourselves forgive everyone who is indebted to us" (v. 4a). You can even pray about your future trials: "And lead us not into temptation" (v. 4b). God cares about every season of your life—past, present, and future.

These petitions teach us how to pray about personal matters. We are to pray as if everything depends on God. For instance, Jesus teaches us to pray for daily bread. We live in a time and place where food is much more accessible than in the days of Jesus. But the fact remains that you will not eat your next meal without God. It all depends on God. Dependence upon God is not a license to be slothful in your work, unrepentant in your sins, or carefree in your lifestyle. Remember, God feeds the birds, but He does not put worms in their nests. The birds have to scratch them up for themselves. Likewise, God's faithfulness does not cancel out your responsibility. You cannot do it without God. But God won't do it without you. You must work as if everything depends on you. But you must pray as if everything depends on God.

PRAY WITH DEPENDENCE UPON GOD

In Luke 11:5–8, Jesus teaches the disciples to pray with dependence by telling the parable of the friend at midnight.

A certain man received an unexpected guest in the middle of the night. The unexpected guest was on a journey. But nightfall caught up with him. He had nowhere to stay, and his resources were depleted. So he turned to a friend who lived in the area. When the unexpected guest arrived, the host warmly welcomed him. "My house is your house," he said. But as he made his unexpected guest comfortable, the host found himself in a crisis of hospitality. There was no food in the house, and the marketplace would remain closed until morning. But the host didn't panic. He excused himself and went to a neighbor's house to borrow a couple of loaves until morning.

Not thinking about the lateness of the hour, this midnight caller knocked on his neighbor's door for help. "Who is it?" growled the voice on the other side of the door. The midnight caller identified himself and explained his dilemma—the unexpected guest, the empty breadbasket, the closed marketplace. The midnight caller was sure these facts would spring his friend into action. He was wrong.

"Leave me alone," barked the sleepy friend. "It has been a long day. The door is locked for the night. My family is in bed with me. I cannot get up and give you anything. Come back in the morning." The sleepy friend then stopped talking. He did not think he needed to say anything else to get the midnight caller to go away.

He was wrong. The midnight caller knocked again. And again. Then louder. He didn't stop. It was as if he was trying to wake up the whole neighborhood, not just his sleepy friend. It was an embarrassing display for both the midnight caller and the sleepy friend. Someone had to put an end to this. So the sleepy friend got out of bed and gave his neighbor several loaves of bread. But he did not do it out of friendship. He bribed the midnight caller with bread. He paid off this shameless neighbor with loaves, so he could get back to sleep. He was willing to give anything he had at the godforsaken hour just to get back to sleep.

This is not a pretty story. But it teaches an important lesson about prayer. Effective prayer requires steadfast dependence upon God. You really cannot pray any other way. In fact, you won't pray without a sense of dependence. Need drives us to God in prayer. It does not matter how much you know about prayer. If you are not aware of your neediness and God's sufficiency, you will never learn to pray. Prayerlessness is a declaration of independence. But needy people pray. The story of the midnight caller and the sleepy friend raises two questions about how your prayer life reveals your level of dependence upon God.

Do you pray? The midnight caller received an unexpected visit from a friend who was on a journey. But he had nothing to feed his unexpected guest. So he went to his neighbor's house, almost instinctively. He was confident that his neighbor could and would supply the bread he needed. Is this what you do in prayer? When you have a problem you cannot solve, do you pray about it? When your friends come to you with a need, do you pray about it? When it is midnight in your life, do you pray about it? Do you give up? Do you try to face the problem on your own? Or do you pray?

Prayerlessness is a declaration of independence. But needy people pray.

Early African-American converts to Christianity would pick specific places for prayer in the fields where they labored as slaves. They spent so much time on their knees in prayer that the grass no longer grew in that spot. And their knees made deep impressions in the soil. These open prayer closets also became points of accountability. When anyone neglected prayer, it was obvious. Eventually, someone would say to his brother, "The grass grows on your path out yonder." Is your place of prayer marked by the impression of your time spent in communion with God? Or has the grass grown on your path out yonder? Do you pray?

I am not talking about some quick, halfhearted, emergency prayer. I'm talking about earnest, diligent, persistent prayer. Do you have a sense of dependence upon God that causes you to knock on the door until you get what you need?

How do you pray? This is the big question the parable of the friend at midnight raises. It does not simply exhort us to pray. It teaches us to pray in a manner that will open closed doors. The key to the parable is in Luke 11:8. Jesus says, "I tell you, though he will not get up and give him anything because he is his friend, yet because of his impudence he will rise and give him whatever he needs." The word "impudence" unlocks the meaning of this parable. The King James Version translates it "importunity." The New King James Version translates it "persistence." And the New International Version translates it "boldness." The Greek word simply means to be without shame. Scholars disagree about who this term applies to—the midnight caller or the sleepy friend. I believe the context of the passage and the message of the parable makes it clear that the term refers to the midnight caller.

Picture the scene again. It was past midnight. The sleepy friend was in bed with his family behind a locked door. And a clear statement like, "Leave me alone," is hard to misunderstand. Common sense, good manners, and personal respect should have made the midnight caller give up when his sleepy friend said he would not, could not help him But shamelessness made the midnight caller continue to knock. He had a need. A guest showed up unexpectedly.

It was late at night. There was no bread in his house. The market was closed. And his sleepy friend was the only one who could supply what he needed. So there was no shame in his game. It didn't matter if he woke up everyone in town. He was determined to keep knocking until his sleepy friend opened the door and gave him the bread he needed.

This is how Jesus wants you to pray. Shamelessly. Sinful pride murders believing prayer. You will never take prayer seriously as long as you are looking for face-saving alternatives to get your needs met. You cannot seek God's face and save your face at the same time. Could this be why God allows you to have an unexpected guest with an empty pantry in the middle of the night? Life is easy when guests schedule their arrival and the market is open in the middle of the day. It is also easy then to forget where your help comes from. But the unexpected forces us to humble ourselves and seek God for what only He can provide.

The midnight caller went to his neighbor's house for bread at an inopportune time. And he did not leave until he had what he needed. His sleepy friend initially refused to help. But he kept knocking until his sleepy friend got up and gave him what he needed. The point of the parable is made by way of contrast. God is the opposite of this story's antihero. Jesus is teaching that God is not a sleepy friend. The psalmist sings, "He will not let your foot be moved; he who keeps you will not slumber. Behold, he who keeps Israel will neither slumber nor sleep" (Psalm 121:3–4). If a sleepy friend will meet the need of his bothersome neighbor just so he can get back to sleep, how much more will our God meet your

needs when you pray! The persistent requests of the midnight caller
worked with the sleepy friend because they bothered him. But your
continual prayer works because it honors the Father in heaven.

One hot afternoon, a certain woman walked to her neighbor's
produce stand to buy grapes. The line was long. And each person
seemed to get special attention. But she waited patiently. When
she finally made it to the front of the line, the owner asked for
her order. She asked for grapes. "Please excuse me for a minute,"
was the answer. Then the owner walked away and disappeared
behind a building. For some reason, this rubbed the woman the
wrong way. Everyone in line before her was greeted warmly. They
were given special attention. And, most importantly, they were
served immediately. But she was forced to
wait. And when she got to the front of the
line, she was forced to wait some more. She
was offended. She felt the owner took her
regular business for granted. The longer she
waited, the angrier she became.

Don't allow your heart to become angry, impatient, or bitter as you wait on God. And don't stop praying.

Finally, the produce stand owner re-
appeared. And with a big smile, he pre-
sented her with the most beautiful grapes she had ever seen. He
invited her to taste them. She had never tasted grapes so good. As
she turned to leave with her delicious grapes, he stopped her. "Oh
yeah, I'm sorry I kept you waiting," said the farmer. "But I needed
the time to get you my very best."

How long have you been in line waiting on God to get to your
request? How long have you been in line waiting for God to answer

your prayer? How long have you been in line waiting for God to meet a need, solve a problem, or open a door? Whatever you do, don't get out of line. Don't allow your heart to become angry, impatient, or bitter as you wait on God. And don't stop praying. Keep knocking at the door. Wait on God. Trust that God causes all things to work together for the good of those who love him and are called according to his purpose (Romans 8:28).

PRAY WITH CONFIDENCE IN GOD

The parables of Jesus are often open-ended. The story ends. The actors leave the stage. The curtain drops. And you are left alone in an empty theater to wrestle with the meaning of what you just experienced. But that is not the case here. In Luke 11:9–13, Jesus makes the point of the parable absolutely clear. The message of the Parable of the Friend at Midnight is that God is willing and able to answer prayer.

God is able to answer prayer. Concluding the parable, Jesus declares, "I tell you, ask, and it will be given to you; seek, and you will find; knock, and it will be opened to you" (Luke 11:9). The verbs—*ask*, *seek*, and *knock*—are imperatives. They are not optional suggestions. They are divine mandates. Jesus does not recommend prayer for your consideration. He commands us to pray. And these imperatives are in a grammatical emphasis that denotes continual or habitual activity. Literally, Jesus commands us to keep asking and seeking and knocking.

Is it a lack of faith to pray for something more than once? Absolutely not. But it is an act of obedience. Jesus commands us to continuously ask, seek, and knock. In other words, don't stop praying. Pray until you get an answer. Pray until something happens. Pray until you get what you ask. Pray until you find what you seek. Pray until the door is opened.

What should you ask for in prayer? What should you seek in life? What door should you knock on for access? Jesus is not specific. He commands us to ask, seek, and knock. But He does not tell us what to pray for. I believe this means you can pray about anything and everything.

You can pray for forgiveness like David.

You can pray for wisdom like Solomon.

You can pray for healing like Hezekiah.

You can pray for a child like Hannah.

You can pray for deliverance like Jonah.

You can pray for mercy like the ten lepers.

You can pray for salvation like the thief on the cross.

Whatever it is, you can pray with the confidence that God is able to answer your prayer. That is the promise Jesus makes without qualification. Your asking will be rewarded with gracious gifts. Your seeking will be rewarded with spiritual discovery. Your knocking will be rewarded with divine welcome. Jesus even guarantees that your prayers will be answered: "For everyone who asks receives, and the one who seeks finds, and to the one who knocks it will be opened" (Luke 11:10).

What should we make of this blanket promise? Is it true? Does Jesus really mean that God will answer every prayer you pray? Answer: yes and no.

No, every prayer will not be answered the way you want it to be. Remember my sincere, urgent prayer that I might see my father before he died? But God's no is not bad news. It is further proof of the good, holy, and loving purposes of God at work in our lives.

How about you? Have you ever asked God for something that seemed so important or urgent at the time? I have. Several times. Once I asked for a transition. God blessed me where I was. I asked for relief. God used the pressure to strengthen me. Another time I asked for my territory to be enlarged. God taught me to live with my borders. Now, looking back, I recognize how foolish, shortsighted, and unnecessary some of my requests have been. Praise God for the prayers He did not answer the way I wanted!

Praise God for the prayers He did not answer the way I wanted!

Likewise, God will not answer every prayer the way you want Him to. Does a father grant every request his children make? Of course not. The Father knows what is best for His children, even when they do not. And the fact that His children will be angry does not cause God to cave in when the answer should be no.

But let me say it as clearly as I can. God answers prayer. God provides. God heals. God saves. God forgives. God strengthens. God comforts. God delivers. God reconciles. God guides. Your situation may not turn out the way you ask or desire. He may not act when or how you want Him to. But God does answer prayer. God is a wise Father who sometimes refuses what you want to give you what you need. But the Lord is good and you can trust Him to answer your prayers. "There is no such thing as unanswered

prayer," wrote William Barclay. "The answer given may not be the
answer we desired or expected; but even when it is a refusal; it is
the answer of the love and wisdom of God."[1]

God is willing to answer your prayers. Jesus makes His final
point by asking several questions about how good fathers respond
to the needs of their children: "What father among you, if his son
asks him for a fish, will instead of a fish give him a serpent; or if he
asks for an egg, will give him a scorpion?" (Luke 11:11–12). These
rhetorical questions assume negative answers. No caring father
would respond to his son's hunger cries in such a cruel, negligent,
and harmful way. To do so would be a kind of child abuse or child
endangerment. A good father will give his son bread and fish, not a
serpent or scorpion. A good father will give his son five loaves and
two fish, if he can.

Jesus assumes that a good father will take care of his children's
basic needs. None of the disciples would have argued with that
point. Then Jesus closes this lesson on prayer by arguing from the
lesser to the greater: "If you then, who are evil, know how to give
good gifts to your children, how much more will the heavenly
Father give the Holy Spirit to those who ask him!" (Luke 11:13).

Wait a minute. Who is Jesus talking to? He is talking to His
disciples. These are men who have forsaken the world to follow
Him. Yet He calls them evil. By doing so, Jesus asserts the pervasive nature of remaining sin. At our best, we are still corrupted by
sin, polluted by worldliness, and infected with selfishness. We are
saved by grace through faith in Christ alone. But we still have evil
in us that needs to be forsaken, cleansed, and overcome.

However, as evil as we are, we still know how to take care of our children. We provide for our children's needs. We even provide beyond their needs, when we can. We surprise them with undeserved gifts. In contrast, John says, "God is light, and in him is no darkness at all" (1 John 1:5). If evil men know how to give good gifts to their children, how much more will God take care of His blood-adopted children.

In the Sermon on the Mount, Jesus said as much. "If you then, who are evil, know how to give good gifts to you children, how much more will your Father who is in heaven give good things to those who ask him!" he told the crowd (Matthew 7:11). And in Luke 11:13, Jesus specifies one of God's best gifts: "If you then, who are evil, know how to give good gifts to your children, how much more will the heavenly Father give the Holy Spirit to those who ask him?"

Be careful not to misinterpret this verse. Jesus makes this promise *before* His atoning death on the cross, His glorious resurrection from the dead, and His permanent gift of the Holy Spirit on the day of Pentecost. Everyone who lives and trusts in Christ on this side of these redemptive milestones is already a beneficiary of the gift of the Holy Spirit. Paul asserts, "Anyone who does not have the Spirit of Christ does not belong to him" (Romans 8:9). If you do not have the Holy Spirit, you are not saved. You are not a Christian. You do not belong to Christ. But if you are in Christ, the Holy Spirit lives in you. You do not have to do anything to receive the Holy Spirit. He is already there.

Every born-again Christian has all of the Holy Spirit he or she will ever get. But the Holy Spirit is still trying to get all of you! When D. L. Moody was asked if he was filled with the Holy Spirit, he answered, "Yes, but I leak." So do I. So do you. But when you pray, God the Father has the Holy Spirit fill you afresh with all that you need to resist temptation, live obediently, model Christlikeness, love selflessly, and live victoriously.

CHAPTER 3

God Is Not a
Crooked Judge

And will not God give justice to his elect,
who cry to him day and night? Will he delay long over them?

LUKE 18:7

The meaning of some parables is not immediately appar-
ent. That's not the case with the Lord's parable of the unjust
judge.

Luke introduces this parable of Jesus by stating its intended
purpose beforehand: "And he told them a parable to the effect
that they ought always to pray and not lose heart" (Luke 18:1).
Jesus tells this parable because He knows that His disciples will be
tempted to lose heart along the way. And the Lord gives a prescrip-
tion to fill when our faith seem to be losing heart.

The term "lose heart" means to give up, give in, or give out
because of weariness, frustration, or discouragement. It is spiritual

burnout that causes one's faith to become faint. Luke 18:1 is the only place this phrase is found in Luke's writings. But the apostle Paul uses it on several occasions. In 2 Corinthians 4:1, Paul says, "Therefore, having this ministry by the mercy of God, we do not lose heart." Later, in 2 Corinthians 4:16, he concludes, "So we do not lose heart. Though our outer self is wasting away, our inner self is being renewed day by day." He tells believers in Ephesus, "So I ask you not to lose heart over what I am suffering for you, which is your glory" (Ephesians 3:13). He says to Christians in Thessalonica, "As for you, brothers, do not grow weary in doing good" (2 Thessalonians 3:13). And Paul writes to those in the Galatian church, "Let us not grow weary of doing good, for in due season we will reap, if we do not give up" (Galatians 6:9).

The temptation to give up is real and powerful. Every person will inevitably face quitting points in life.

These Bible verses warn us that the temptation to give up is real and powerful and unavoidable. Every person will inevitably face quitting points in life. It does not matter how long you have walked with the Lord, how much Scripture you know, or how deep your level of devotion to the Lord is. "Therefore let anyone who thinks that he stands take heed lest he fall," warns Paul (1 Corinthians 10:12). Be on your guard. You are not immune to losing heart. All of us will face quitting points at some time or another.

FACING THOSE QUITTING POINTS

There are personal quitting points. They appear when you feel like you have given all you can give or that you have taken all you can take. You are at wit's end. You are crushed by the straw that broke the camel's back.

There are relational quitting points. They occur when dealing with someone you care about brings you to that can't-live-with-them-can't-live-without-them point of exasperation. Your relationship is more than strained. It's broken. You feel like you cannot go any further with this person.

There are moral quitting points. They loom ahead when you consider negotiating your values, because doing wrong seems to pay so well and doing right seems to cost too much. Without a doubt, life constantly offers you spiritual shortcuts. And they can seem very inviting when the pressure is on.

Finally, there are spiritual quitting points. These will tempt you when your faith begins to faint and you feel like giving up on God. During a spiritual depression we need to sing with the psalmist, "Why are you cast down, O my soul, and why are you in turmoil within me? Hope in God; for I shall again praise him, my salvation and my God" (Psalm 42:5–6).

THE POWER OF PERSISTENT PRAYER

We all face quitting points in life. The question is: What do you do when you are tempted to lose heart? How should you respond when your faith begins to faint? Is there any counsel from the Lord to face those times when you feel like giving up?

The answer appears in Luke's introduction to Jesus' parable: "And he told them a parable to the effect that they ought always to pray and not lose heart." Did you hear the answer in the words of that verse? Prayer is the remedy for discouragement. Period. You should pray when you begin to lose heart. This is not a recommendation. It is not a suggestion that you can accept or reject at your discretion. It is not optional. The call to prayer is a moral imperative. "They ought always to pray," Luke says. It is wrong to give up at life's quitting points. You must pray your way through.

Of course, this is not an easy thing to do. Such diligence requires more than sporadic, halfhearted, or reactionary prayer. You ought always to pray. You are to continue steadfastly in prayer. You ought to pray until something happens. Diligence defeats discouragement. Continual prayer will keep you from losing heart. Persistent prayer revives the fainting heart. This is why 1 Thessalonians 5:17 exhorts us to "pray without ceasing." What does this mean? Does it mean that you should do nothing but pray? No. It means that you are to do nothing without prayer. Don't take a step without prayer. Don't make a decision without prayer. Don't take a step without prayer. Don't take action without prayer. You ought to always pray and not lose heart.

> **Continual prayer will keep you from losing heart. Persistent prayer revives the fainting heart.**

Jesus illustrates the priority and power of prayer with another parable recorded in Luke 18:2–5:

In a certain city there was a judge who neither feared God nor respected man. And there was a widow in that city that kept coming to him and saying, 'Give me justice against my adversary.' For a while he refused, but afterward he said to himself, 'Though I neither fear God nor respect man, yet because this widow keeps bothering me, I will give her justice, so that she will not beat me down by her continual coming.'

This intriguing little parable has two main characters. First there is a judge, whom Jesus describes as a man "who neither feared God nor respected man." What a stinging indictment! This expression tells us that this man was morally unfit to be a judge. "The fear of the Lord is the beginning of knowledge," teaches Proverbs 1:7; "fools despise wisdom and instruction." As one who did not fear God, how could this man properly administer the law of God?

There are many people today who think one's theology can be separated from one's ethics. In fact, many people act as if the two should never be joined together! But Jesus married the two by telling us that this crooked judge's lack of reverence for God corresponded with his lack of respect for people. I've often heard the statement "I couldn't care less" thrown around by those who don't really mean it. But it was actually the life philosophy of this judge. He literally couldn't care less about God or anyone else. He was a heartless, wicked man whose every verdict was purely motivated by his crooked self-interests.

The other main character of the parable is a widow. And Jesus goes out of His way to describe her in desperate terms. First, she was a woman who lived in the highly chauvinistic culture of the ancient Near East. In a real sense, she had no personal rights. Her existence was tied to men in her life.

Likewise, she was a widow whose position, provision, and protection were all snatched away from her by the death of her husband. And, apparently, she didn't have a father, son, brother, or anyone else to speak up on her behalf.

Furthermore, this poor woman had an adversary who she could not handle on her own. This most likely means that she was entangled in a financial dispute with some man who was taking advantage of her.

Worst of all, this helpless, desperate widow happened to live under the jurisdiction of this unscrupulous judge who neither feared God nor respected people.

> **This widow did not have the power to force the judge to hear her case. But this widow did have something she could use . . . she had persistence.**

So when this desperate loser went to this heartless winner for justice, he flatly refused to help her. Under normal circumstances, this would have been the end of the matter—leaving the widow helpless and hopeless. But the irony of this parable is that the loser wins. This widow did not have the power to force the judge to hear her case. She did not have any powerful connections to influence him. And she did not have any money to bribe him. But this widow did have something she could use to convince the judge to change his mind. In a word, she had persistence.

Imagine the scene. The widow came to the judge's office, seeking justice against her adversary. The judge doesn't just refuse to help; he demeans her and kicks her out. The nerve of such a nobody to think he would act on her behalf! He then gets back to work, plotting further crooked schemes, never expecting to see or hear from this widow again. But when he leaves the office for lunch, there she is, asking for justice. When he returns, she is still there asking for justice. At the end of the day, she follows him home, asking for justice. And when he leaves for work the next day, there she is asking for justice. Unfortunately for this judge, he can't just issue a restraining order against this widow to make her leave him alone. So she keeps bothering him.

Finally, her punishing persistence wears him down and he agrees to hear her case and render justice. Can you hear him? "Will someone please help this old lady, before she knocks me out with unrelenting persistence!"

This is the parable Jesus tells to make the point that His disciples ought always to pray and not lose heart. Prayer is the remedy for discouragement. Persistent prayer revives the fainting heart.

In Luke 18:6–8, Jesus drives the point of this parable home with a series of questions: "Hear what the unrighteous judge says. And will not God give justice to his elect, who cry to him day and night? Will he delay long over them? I tell you, he will give justice to them speedily. Nevertheless, when the Son of Man comes, will he find faith on earth?"

Let's wrestle with the implications of this parable in the same way. Consider these two big questions about the main characters of this parable to help you understand why you ought to always pray and not lose heart.

A KEY QUESTION:
IS GOD LIKE THIS CROOKED JUDGE?

I want to offer two answers to this key question.

Yes, there is a real sense in which God is like this crooked judge. Like the parable of the friend at midnight in Luke 11:5–8, the lesson Jesus teaches about God in this parable is made by way of contrast, not comparison. God is the antithesis of this character. That is, God is not a crooked judge. But this does not mean that there are absolutely no similarities between God and this judge. They are polar opposites in terms of their moral character. But they share the same authoritative role. Both are judges. This unjust judge ruled his jurisdiction. Like it or not, the residents in his jurisdiction had to go to him to receive justice. In terms of ruling authority, God is like this crooked judge. God is sovereign. Divine sovereignty simply means that God is God alone. He rules and reigns over everything. God has absolute control, complete authority, and unimpeachable jurisdiction over all creation. Ultimately, God is the only being that truly has free will. Everything and everyone is subject to God's sovereign authority.

So here is a real sense in which God is like this crooked judge. God is in charge. The psalmist declares, "Our God is in the heavens; he does all that he pleases" (Psalm 115:3). And we must turn to God for justice. God is the only one who can make it right when things go wrong in our lives. This is the distinct nuance between the two parables Jesus teaches on the subject of believing prayer. The parable of the friend at midnight teaches that God will meet your needs if you pray. But the parable of the unjust judge teaches that God will fix your problems if you pray. When things go wrong, you don't have to give up, give in, or give out. And you don't have to take matters into your own hands. God has everything under control.

When things go wrong, you don't have to give up, give in, or give out.

Ultimately, God is not like this crooked judge. The unjust judge decides to help the widow, "so that she will not beat me down by her continual coming," he says (Luke 18:5). In this statement, the crooked judge uses a term that means to give someone a black eye. That's how this widow got her way with this judge. She beat him down with her nagging and unrelenting persistence. He finally decided to help her just to get her off his back. Herein lies the tension of the text—the contrast between this crooked judge and our heavenly Father. God is not a crooked judge. You have critically misunderstood both God and prayer if you think that prayer is about bugging God long enough or nagging God hard enough that you wear Him down to get your needs met.

"We must not conceive of Prayer as overcoming God's reluctance," wrote Richard Trench, "but as laying hold of his highest willingness."[1] You ought always to pray and not lose heart because God is not a crooked judge.

OUR GOOD AND JUST GOD

This judge, who neither feared God nor respected man, was a stubborn, hardhearted man who was only motivated by crooked self-interests. But our God is a good God. James 1:17 says, "Every good gift and every perfect gift is from above, coming down from the Father of lights with whom there is no variation or shadow due to change." God does not shift or turn or change. And nothing that does shift or turn or change can eclipse God's goodness. God is good all the time. *God's character is good*. And God's ways never contradict His character. God only and always does what is good. This is true no matter how bad things may get in your life. Indeed, life is hard. But God is still good. The goodness of God always outweighs the badness of life. So you can pray with confidence, knowing that God's character is good.

Besides His good character, *God's ways are just*. To say that God is just is to say that God judges by a righteous standard. In this sense, God is no respecter of persons. God's judgments are not shaped by our comparisons, excuses, or rationalizations in any way. God doesn't grade on a curve. God judges by a righteous standard: namely, His own good and holy character. If you want proof of the justness of God, run to the cross. There behold the miracle of divine justice, in which God demonstrated His unconditional love without violating His holy wrath. On the cross, God treated Jesus as if He had committed all of our sins so He could treat those who believe as if they had performed all of the righteousness of Christ (2 Corinthians 5:21). This is the miracle of the sacrificial and subsitutionary death of Jesus that satisfies the justice of God.

Romans 8:32 rightly asks: "He who did not spare his own Son but gave him up for us all, how will he not also with him graciously give us all things?" In other words, if you can trust the justice of God to save you, you ought to trust God to sustain you, protect you, and keep you. The God who has settled your eternal destiny also oversees your daily experience. The Lord who has prepared an eternal home for you will get you safely there. "And whom he predestined he also called, and those whom he called he also justified, and those whom he justified he also glorified" (Romans 8:30). There is no need to worry. God will take care of you.

> **Behold the miracle of divine justice, in which God demonstrated His unconditional love without violating His holy wrath.**

Besides God's good character and just ways, *God's timing is perfect*. Jesus asks, "And will not God give justice to his elect, who cry to him day and night? Will he delay long over them?" (Luke 18:7). This statement has proven difficult for scholars to interpret and translate. Literally, the Greek suggests that God may delay His coming or tarry long with His elect. But in verse 8, Jesus says, "I tell you, he will give justice to them speedily." Well which is it? Does He tarry? Or does He come speedily? It is both. There are times when God forces you to sit in His waiting room. But when He acts on your behalf, He moves speedily.

God's timing is perfect. This truth brings great comfort to my soul. God is never in a hurry. God is from everlasting to everlasting (Psalm 90:2). God lives in one eternal now. He is not bound by clocks and calendars. It really doesn't matter when the Lord shows up. It's always the right time. He showed up for Noah years before the flood. But it was the right time. He showed up for Shadrach, Meshach, and Abednego while they were in the fiery furnace. But it was still the right time. He did not show up for Mary and Martha until after Lazarus had been dead for four days. But it was still the right time. "Too late" is not in God's vocabulary. God knows how to act. God knows where to act. And God knows when to act.

A SECOND KEY QUESTION:
ARE YOU LIKE THE PERSISTENT WIDOW?

Let me offer three answers to this question.

Yes, there is a real sense in which you are like this widow. This poor widow went to the crooked judge and pleaded, "Give me justice against my adversary" (Luke 18:3). She had an enemy who she could not handle on her own. Likewise, you and I have an enemy who we cannot handle on our own. This widow was probably in a financial dispute with some man who had taken advantage of her. But our conflict is a spiritual dispute with eternal implications in which we struggle against the enemies of our souls—the flesh, the world, and the Devil—that seek to take advantage of us. It's a war on terror that demands that highest level of alert.

Here's the terror plot. The flesh wants you to be happy. The world wants you to fit in. And the Devil wants you to be religious. Admittedly, these things don't sound very threatening. But the underlying danger lies in the fact that the flesh wants you to be happy without God. The world wants you to fit in without God. And the Devil wants you to be religious without God.

The temptation to live without God at the center of your life is our spiritual enemy's weapon of mass destruction. The adversary knows that you cannot handle him on your own. So he constantly schemes to undermine your faith in God. In fact, the Enemy wants you to believe that God is a crooked judge so that you won't pray. If you don't pray, the Enemy is assured the victory. You are like this widow in that you have an adversary that you cannot handle on your own.

However, if you are in Christ, you are not like this desperate widow. Jesus asks, "And will not God give justice to his elect, who cry to him day and night?" (Luke 18:7). The word "elect" is precious. It means to be chosen by God. *Election* describes the process of salvation from a divine and eternal perspective. It means that you are saved because God chose you, not because you chose God. It was God's choosing of you that enabled you to choose Him. Thus, those who are saved are God's elect. That's what you are in Jesus Christ. You are God's chosen one.

> **Elect means to be chosen by God. Election describes the process of salvation from a divine and eternal perspective.**

Ephesians 1:3–4 says, "Blessed be the God and Father of our Lord Jesus Christ, who has blessed us in Christ with every spiritual blessing in the heavenly places, even as he chose us in him before the foundation of the word, that we should be holy and blameless before him." God has chosen you for Himself in Christ. In fact, before God said, "Let there be light," He had you on His mind! As one of God's chosen ones, you have been placed in a position of complete spiritual blessing. So you are free to come to God as one of His elect, not as some helpless widow.

As God's elect, you have direct access to God. This widow didn't have any real access to the judge. Even though he was the judge over her jurisdiction, she had no reason to believe that he would listen to a nobody like her. Unless you could do something to benefit him, this judge didn't have time for you. But that is not the Christian's predicament. Prayer is not a scheduled appointment with a busy executive. It is quality time with a loving Father. You and I have complete access to God through faith in Jesus Christ. We can come boldly and with confidence to the throne of grace to receive grace and mercy when we need it (Hebrews 4:16).

Likewise, as God's elect, you have an advocate before God. This widow did not have anybody to speak to the judge on her behalf—not a husband, not a father, not a son. No one. But you and I have a mediator who intercedes on our behalf before God. John the apostle writes, "If anyone does sin, we have an advocate with the Father, Jesus Christ the righteous" (1 John 2:1). An "advocate" is a defense attorney. He speaks on the behalf of the accused. When the accuser of the brethren speaks against you (Revelation 12:10), your divine Advocate speaks on your behalf, pleading His blood on your behalf. Really, the fix is in—a *good* fix for our would-be problem. God the Father is the Judge. And the Lord Jesus Christ, our elder Brother, is our defense. And so Paul declares, "Who shall bring any charge against God's elect? It is God who justifies. Who is to condemn? Christ Jesus is the one who died—more than that, who was raised—who is at the right hand of God, who indeed is interceding for us" (Romans 8:33–34).

Break out of your widow mentality! Remember you are God's elect.

Furthermore, as God's elect, you have assurance from God. This widow did not have any agreement with this judge that would obligate him to do anything for her. How could she, dealing with someone who did not fear God or respect men? With

When the accuser of the brethren speaks against you, your divine Advocate speaks on your behalf, pleading His blood on your behalf.

this crooked judge, seeing was the only way to believe him. You couldn't take him at his word. He was as sure to change his mind as the wind is to blow in a different direction. But this is not how our God operates. Balaam was right: "God is not man, that he should lie, or a son of man, that he should change his mind. Has he said, and will he not do it? Or has he spoken, and will he not fulfill it?" (Numbers 23:19).

You and I have the faithful promises of almighty God to appeal to as we cry out to Him for help. "His divine power has granted to us all things that pertain to life and godliness, through the knowledge of him who called us to his own glory and excellence, by which he has granted to us his precious and very great promises, so that through them you may become partakers of the divine nature, having escaped from the corruption that is in the world because of sinful desire" (2 Peter 1:3–4). Praise God! We can take God at His word. We can trust the Lord to do what He says. We can stand on the promises of Christ our King.

Are you like this desperate widow? Let me give you one more

answer to ponder: I don't know. Really, I don't know. For Jesus turns the parable of the unjust judge on its head with a closing question: "Nevertheless, when the Son of Man comes, will he find faith on earth?" (Luke 18:8b).

Be clear; Jesus did not ask this question out of ignorance. If such faith is to be found, Jesus is the only one who can find it. Likewise, Jesus did not ask this question in despair. The Son of Man will find faith on the earth when He comes again. It may only be a remnant of humanity. But it will yet be a great congregation assembled from every nation, tribe, tongue, and people group on the earth. Nor is Jesus predicting a worldwide apostasy in the last days.

Rather, this is a spiritual challenge that each of us must face. As you read through this passage, the question of the parable seems to be whether the Lord will show up when His elect need Him. But now this parable is telling us the real question is not whether the Lord will show up. The real question is, Will you show up when He shows up? Are you like this persistent widow? Will you persist in prayer? Or will you lose heart? Will you give up and throw in the towel before the Lord brings justice to you speedily? When the Son of Man comes, will He find faith on earth?

Jesus predicts, "And because lawlessness will be increased, the love of many will grow cold. But the one who endures to the end will be saved" (Matthew 24:12–13). Of course, it is not enduring that saves. Salvation is a gift we receive, not a reward we earn (Ephesians 2:8–9). But steadfast endurance is the distinguishing mark of those who are truly saved. "And I am sure of this," Paul testifies, "that he who began a good work in you will bring it to completion at the day of Jesus Christ" (Philippians 1:6). God is going to do His part. But you must do your part.

The fact is we are so weak, limited, and sinful that we need God to help us do our part as well. And He has made provision to help us. He has given us the wonderful privilege of prayer. Will your love grow cold? Or will you endure to the end? You can endure to the end if you always pray and do not lose heart.

CHAPTER 4

The Wise Prayer of a
Weak Man

Two things I ask of you; deny them not to me before I die.

PROVERBS 30:7

You can learn a lot about a person by listening to him or her pray.

In this chapter, we'll learn about a man named Agur through his prayer recorded in Proverbs 30:7–9, which begins, "Two things I ask of you; deny them not to me before I die: Remove far from me falsehood and lying; give me neither poverty nor riches; feed me with the food that is needful for me."

Agur is mentioned only once in the Bible (Proverbs 30:1). Speculation is that Agur is a pseudonym under which Solomon, the author of most of the proverbs, wrote. But we cannot know for sure. Who was Agur? All we can know comes from the contents of Proverbs 30. Yet there is much we can learn about this obscure personality from his wise sayings. And the most important things about Agur are revealed in the wise prayer of this weak man. Agur's intercession teaches us several important lessons about prayer, before we ever get to the main petitions of the prayer.

LESSON 1: PRAY WITH HUMBLE SUBMISSION

"Two things I ask of you," Agur begins, adding, "deny them not to me before I die" (Proverbs 30:7). Consider how Agur made his requests to the Lord. Agur *asked* God for two things. This is an important detail. He did not tell the Lord what to do. He did not claim any promises. He did not use the force of faith. He did not write his own ticket with God. He did not try to manipulate God to produce his desired reality.

Without a doubt, Agur's prayer is earnest and urgent. Yet Agur simply asked God for what he wanted—like a servant addressing a master, like a child talking to his father, like a sinful man addressing a holy God. This is how we should approach God in prayer, with humble submission, not arrogant presumption.

LESSON 2: PRAY WITH SPIRITUAL PRIORITIES

Agur did not pray for foolish, trivial, or superficial things. Rather, his prayer carried the weight of eternity: "Two things I ask of you; deny them not to me *before I die*" (emphasis added). Think about that. As Agur prayed about his life he was thinking about his death. Moses prayed, "So teach us to number our days that we may get a heart of wisdom" (Psalm 90:12). By this standard, we can conclude that Agur was a wise-hearted man. He numbered his days. He was in touch with his mortality. He lived in light of eternity. He did not lay up treasure on earth (see Matthew 6:19). He recognized it is appointed for every person to die and stand before God in judgment (Hebrews 9:27). So Agur prayed with a life-and-death focus.

> **When you pray, remember that life is short. Death is sure. Eternity is long. Don't major on minor things in prayer.**

Our prayers should also bear the weight of our inevitable date with eternity. "In praying," wrote Matthew Henry, "we should think of dying, and pray accordingly." This is great advice. Worldly prayer does not reach heaven. When you pray, remember that God is sovereign. Life is short. Death is sure. Hell is real. Eternity is long. Don't major on minor things in prayer. "But seek first the kingdom of God and his righteousness," instructs Jesus, "and all these things will be added to you" (Matthew 6:33).

LESSON 3: PRAY WITH GODLY WISDOM

"If any of you lacks wisdom," instructs James, "let him ask God, who gives generously to all without reproach, and it will be given to him" (James 1:5). What a privilege. We can pray to God for wisdom when we need it. And God will freely provide spiritual wisdom, without chastising you for asking. We should pray for wisdom. But we should also pray *with* wisdom. This is another lesson Agur teaches us.

Agur apparently processed things in organized lists. His prayer is the first and shortest of six numerical lists in Proverbs 30. In this prayer list, Agur strategically asked God for just two things. Agur would not have dared go before an ancient dignitary without a specific purpose and thoughtful preparation. All the more, Agur prayed intentionally. He would not thoughtlessly or carelessly go into the presence of God. He did not pray a long, vague, rambling prayer. Agur prayed intentionally, specifically, and purposefully. William Arnot described Agur's precise petitions as "a sharp reproof of every dim word-cloud that floats above men's heads, and calls itself a prayer."[1] Agur knew what he wanted in life. And he confidently but reverently brought his requests to the one who is willing to hear and able to answer prayer.

Let me ask you something. If you were to make a prayer list of the things you want God to do for you before you die, how long would your list be? What would be on your list? Would that list show you to be wise or foolish?

Agur had a very short list. It consisted of only two requests that reflect godly wisdom. He asked God to take away the things in his life that blocked his pursuit of godliness. Then he asked God not to give him anything that would detour him from his pursuit of godliness. That's it. That's the prayer of Agur. Interestingly, this is the only prayer recorded in Proverbs. One may conclude from this that this prayer succinctly summarizes how wise, godly people pray. I commend this prayer to you to face and overcome the things in your life that challenge the development of godliness in your life. To be like Jesus, pray like Agur.

LESSON 4: ASK GOD TO REMOVE THE THINGS THAT
BLOCK YOUR PURSUIT OF GODLINESS

The development of a godly life requires a firm commitment to divine truth. Christ followers must live truth-driven lives. Jesus said, "If you abide in my word, you are truly my disciples, and you will know the truth, and the truth will set you free" (John 8:31–32). During His high-priestly prayer, Jesus prayed for His disciples, "Sanctify them in the truth; your word is truth" (John 17:17).

This is where Agur starts his prayer: "Remove far from me falsehood and lies" (v. 7). There are two concerns here.

Deceitful speech. The word "falsehood" refers to that which is empty. It is that which is without value or meaning. The same Hebrew word is used in the third Commandment: "You shall not take the name of the Lord your God in vain, for the Lord will not hold him guiltless who takes his name in vain" (Exodus 20:7). Vanity is falsehood. It is that which is empty, meaningless, or worthless.

Agur prays against falsehood. He confronts the deceitful act of saying something you do not mean in order to take advantage of another person. Deceitful speech is unbecoming for godly people. Peter lists deceit as one of the things we must strip off once and for all if we are to desire the pure spiritual milk of the word and to grow up in the faith (1 Peter 2:1). Likewise, Peter tells us that Jesus is qualified to be our Savior because He committed no sin and there was no deceit found in His mouth (v. 22). Praise God! Everything Jesus says is true. And He is our righteous standard. As followers of the Lord Jesus, we must get rid of falsehood.

Dishonest speech. Falsehood and lies are twins. But they are not identical twins. Lies are uglier than falsehood. Did you know that a person who speaks falsehood might actually be speaking truth? This person has no personal commitment to that spoken truth.

Everything Jesus says is true. As followers of the Lord Jesus, we must get rid of falsehood.

Such a person is a hypocrite, both implying to support the truth when he does not and pretending to be something before others that he is not before God. Ironically, the pretense of the hypocrite is a backwards acknowledgment of the objective standard of truth. By his falsehood, the hypocrite acts as if he is aligned with the truth. However, a liar does not acknowledge the truth in any way. He has no respect for the truth in his heart, and he has no respect for the truth in his words. Liars despise the truth. No wonder the wise man said, "Lying lips are an abomination to the Lord" (Proverbs 12:22a). God hates liars.

So Agur wisely prays, "Remove far from me falsehood and lies."

What is Agur talking about? The meaning of this request is clear. The context is not. Agur could be praying for a personal commitment to truth. There may be a confession of sin imbedded within this prayer request. He may be acknowledging his sinful habit of speaking falsehood and lies from which he needs God to deliver him. Or this prayer request may be a declaration of war against the powerful temptation to speak falsehood and lies that constantly attacked Agur's faith. If so, Agur's request would convey the spirit of Jesus' model prayer that instructs us to pray, "Lead us not into temptation" (Matthew 6:13). Agur may be asking God for victory over the seductive, nagging temptation to speak falsehood and lies.

The problem, however, may not have been within Agur. It may have been around him. In Proverbs 30:5–6, Agur asserts: "Every word of God proves true; he is a shield to those who take refuge in him. Do not add to his words, lest he rebuke you and you be found a liar." After this stern warning, Agur prays that God would remove falsehood and lies far away from him. The connection of these two proverbs suggests that Agur may have been plagued with people in his life who spoke falsehood and lies. Can you relate?

More specifically, they may have been people who did not rightly handle the word of truth (2 Timothy 2:15). They misinterpreted and misrepresented Scripture to make the Word of God say what it does not mean. Such people are a clear and present danger to godly faith. So Agur did not just want God to ultimately rebuke these people; he wanted God to immediately remove them from his life.

We do not know which reading of the text most accurately reflects Agur's intentions. But either way you read this petition, the point is the same. Agur prayed for deliverance from falsehood and lies, because he was too weak to deal with these issues by himself. His good intentions couldn't do it. His strategic plans couldn't do it. His best efforts couldn't do it. Only God could produce the commitment to the truth that Agur desired. Falsehood and lies were malicious termites that ate away at the foundation and structure of truth in Agur's life. He could not fully identify his vulnerable points or the extent of the threat, much less deal with it on his own. So he called on the sovereign "Exterminator," asking God to remove falsehood and lies from his life.

So vulnerable was Agur that he asked God to remove falsehood and lies "far" from him. He didn't want them to be removed yet remain nearby. Falsehood and lies may come back to get him again. Or worse, he may go and get them! Remember, you can easily fall out of bed if you lay too close to where you got in. So Agur prayed, "Remove far from me falsehood and lies."

When I was a boy I had a tree house in the backyard; it sat on top of a play system, with a slide and swings. There was a long ladder my friends and I would climb to get to reach it. One day, as my friend Shawn and I were going up the stairs, my leg became stuck. Caught there on the stairs, I could not free myself. Shawn climbed up to help me, but could not help me break free.

Agur prayed for deliverance from falsehood and lies, because he was too weak to deal with these issues by himself.

Panicking, I screamed, "Go get my daddy!"

Shawn ran into the house and retrieved my dad. He was like a superhero showing up on the scene to save the day. I will not forget how he climbed up to rescue me that day. Unlike Shawn and me, my dad did not try to pull my leg free. Instead he began ripping the steps from the ladder. Then he carried me down to safety. He made sure I was okay and then went back into the house. Shawn and I resumed playing, as if nothing had happened. But when there was a break in the action, I noticed Shawn staring at me. I asked him what was wrong.

"Boy, your dad is strong!" he said.

Are you stuck? Does something in your life have you bound? Has your spiritual progress been impeded? You may have been trying to break free for a long time. Family and friends have tried to help, but have proven unable to deliver you. Resources that you once thought were so valuable have proven unhelpful, as well. Is that you? Then I have good news to give you. Our Father in heaven is strong! His grace is all you need and His strength works best in weak people (2 Corinthians 12:9). And there is nothing you are into that the Lord cannot get you out of! Just ask God to remove whatever it is in your life that blocks your pursuit of godliness.

LESSON 5: ASK GOD TO BLOCK THOSE THINGS
THAT DETOUR YOUR PURSUIT OF GODLINESS

First Chronicles 4:9–10 records the prayer of another obscure biblical personality named Jabez. We don't really know much about Jabez outside of this prayer. But as Agur has shown, you can learn a lot about a person by listening to him or her pray. So listen to Jabez's prayer. He asked God to richly bless him and expand his borders. But as he asked God for more territory, Jabez recognized the inherent danger of his prayer request. So he also asked that the hand of God would be with him to keep him from evil.

The prayer of Agur is the counterpart to the prayer of Jabez. Jabez prayed for God's strengthening power to maintain his integrity after he received the blessings he desired—a good thing. Agur said, "I'm too weak to pray like that!" Instead, he asked God not to grant him any blessing that would expose his weakness, compromise his values, or put his integrity in jeopardy—also a good thing. "Give me neither poverty nor riches," he prayed. "Feed me with the food that is needful for me, lest I be full and deny you and say, 'Who is the Lord?' or lest I be poor and steal and profane the name of my God" (Proverbs 30:8b–9).

Agur's petition is more extensive than Jabez's, and it neatly divides into two parts. First, Agur asks the Lord not to give him poverty. At first glance, this does not seem to be a very profound prayer request. I think it's safe to say that we don't really want to be poor. In fact, comparable to many other countries in the world, most of us don't even know what real poverty looks like.

> **Money is amoral. A wealthy person can be godly, selfless, and generous. And a poor person can be worldly, selfish, and greedy.**

Ultimately, money is amoral. It is neither good nor bad. The fact is a wealthy person can be godly, selfless, and generous. And a poor person can be worldly, selfish, and greedy. The difference has nothing to do with what one does or does not have. It is all about your attitude toward material possessions. The prayer of Agur warns us that being poor can have a corrupting influence in your life.

There is no particular virtue in being poor, Agur argues. So he prays that God would not give him poverty.

The first part of this request makes sense. Do not give me poverty. But the second part of this prayer request is the hard part for many people to swallow: Do not give me riches (v. 8). Most of us do not outright ask for riches any more than we ask for poverty. Yet our hearts desire more income, affluence, and possessions—

not less. D. L. Moody wisely taught, "Getting riches brings care; keeping them brings trouble; abusing them brings guilt, and losing them brings sorrow. It is a great mistake to make so much of riches as we do."[2] Yet far too many of us make the big mistake of making too much of riches. We know the axiom, "The more money you get the more problems you have." But the potential problems money brings do not dissuade us from pursuing wealth—even when it causes spiritual problems. We just conclude that we'll cross that bridge when we get to it.

The contemporary church in America desperately needs to hear and heed Paul's admonition to Timothy: "Those who desire to be rich fall into temptation, into a snare, into many senseless and harmful desires that plunge people into ruin and destruction. For the love of money is a root of all kinds of evils. It is through this craving that some have wandered away from the faith and pierced themselves through with many pangs" (1 Timothy 6:9–10). Beware: material prosperity can become a cancer to the soul.

Agur's prayer request makes an important theological assertion: God is the ultimate source of both poverty and riches. Have you considered that? In asking God not to give him poverty or riches, Agur acknowledges that whichever one he receives comes from God. Paul rightly proclaimed that God "gives to all mankind life and breath and everything" (Acts 17:25). Yes, everything comes from God, whether it is good or bad. You may not like the thought of that. Honestly, it rubs me the wrong way, too. But the alternatives are even more distasteful. If God does not have sovereign control over all creation, history, and circumstances, it would mean that things happen by chance, accident, or dumb luck. Or worse, it would mean that Satan is free to do whatever he wants to do in the world, without God knowing or being able to do anything about it. Or worst of all, it would mean that our destiny is in our own hands. God forbid!

The good news is that God is in control of everything. He is in the heavens, doing whatever pleases Him (Psalm 115:3). And I didn't learn that from reading Martin Luther or John Calvin or Jonathan Edwards. I learned that in the children's choir in the church where I grew up. We learned to sing (in three different verses), "He's got the whole world in His hands. . . . He's got the little, bitty baby in His hands. . . . He's got you and me, brother, in His hands." Hallelujah! It's all in His hands, be it poverty or riches. So even when you don't like the gift, remember how good and wise and great the Giver is. Trust that Romans 8:28 is still true: "And we know that for those who love God all things work together for good, for those who are called according to his purpose."

> **Proverbs warns against the danger of extremes. Godly wisdom leads to a balanced life.**

The fact that Agur prayed for neither poverty nor riches does not mean that he did not want any material possessions. The wisdom of Proverbs warns against the danger of extremes. Godly wisdom leads to a balanced life. And Agur demonstrates this fundamental element of godly wisdom by asking the Lord to keep him from both poverty and riches: "give me neither poverty nor riches; feed me with the food that is needful for me" (v. 8).

Agur makes this prayer request in both negative and positive terms. The positive statement clarifies the negative statement. Agur addressed his concern about the danger of poverty and riches by asking God to give him the food that was needful for him. The New International Version translates the end of verse 8: "Give me only my daily bread." This is a clear allusion to the Model Prayer, where Jesus taught His disciples to pray, "Give us this day our daily bread" (Matthew 6:11).

For many in Jesus' day, their entire meal consisted of bread. They could not afford anything else. Bread was all they had. And this is what Jesus taught His disciples to ask for. Just bread. And He doesn't want them to have bread stored up for days to come. He instructs them to ask for daily bread. Praying simply for bread every day keeps the heart in a posture of humility and dependence before God. It forces us to acknowledge that the things we need to survive do not show up automatically. They come from an outside Source. And if that Source does not provide for us, we will die.

> **Praying for bread every day keeps us in humility before God. It forces us to acknowledge that what we need to survive does not show up automatically.**

Do you get it? Praying for daily bread is meant to help us remember that we need God. And we do not just need God to show up on certain days, as if we could make it without Him at other times. We need God's gracious provisions "this day" and "daily." There is not a time in our lives when we do not need God.

This is the heart of Agur's request. He is asking God to keep him in a posture of dependence. He is asking God to help him to remember that he needs God every day. He is asking God to work in his life in a way that would force him to walk by faith and not by sight.

Why pray this way? Agur explains, ". . . lest I be full and deny you and say, 'Who is the Lord?' or lest I be poor and steal and profane the name of my God" (Proverbs 30:9). Agur understood that life is not defined by material possessions. Jesus said, "Take care, and be on your guard against all covetousness, for one's life does not consist in the abundance of his possessions" (Luke 12:15). Let that sink in.

You are more than the amount of money you have in the bank.

You are more than the kind of car you drive.

You are more than the neighborhood you live in.

You are more than the type of work you do.

Life is about more than the things you possess. True life consists of a right relationship with God. The preacher rightly concluded, "The end of the matter; all has been heard. Fear God and keep his commandments, for this is the whole duty of man. For God will bring every deed into judgment, with every secret thing, whether good or evil" (Ecclesiastes 12:13–14). So Agur prayed that he would not receive anything that would hinder his relationship with God. "Wealth is desired or dreaded, not for its own sake," comments William Arnot, "but as it might serve to help or hinder the progress of grace in the soul."[3]

LESSON 6: ASK GOD TO GIVE YOU THE RIGHT ATTITUDE ABOUT PROSPERITY, SO YOU WILL NOT DENY HIM

In the book of Job, Satan asserted that Job only served God because of God's blessings on his life (Job 1:6–12). He wagered that if Job's circumstances changed, Job would curse God, rather than serve Him. Satan was wrong about Job. But he was right about people. Some people only serve God because of the blessings they receive.

Agur's prayer is the other side of the story. Agur did not want to be full. He did not believe in financial independence. He did not strive for financial security. He looked beyond the benefits of wealth and focused on the deceitfulness of riches, asking God not to give him riches that would make Agur "full and deny [Him] and say 'Who is the Lord?'" (v. 9a).

An empty stomach reminds us of our need for God. But a full stomach can create a false sense of self-sufficiency. Material wealth may lead to spiritual indifference. Agur understood the peril of prosperity and did not want this to happen to him. He did not want to become full and start asking, "Who is the Lord?" Don't misunderstand what this question

> **A full stomach can create a false sense of self-sufficiency. Material wealth may lead to spiritual indifference.**

means. It is not a sincere request for the knowledge of God. It is a sarcastic denial of God's authority that suggests that one does not need God if their stomach is full. It is blasphemous sarcasm of foolish pride that does not recognize where its help comes from.

Moses warned the children of Israel about this danger in his valedictorian speech as a nation of people had completed their course and were ready to enter the land God had promised:

> Take care lest you forget the Lord your God by not keeping his commandments and his rules and his statutes, which I command you today, lest, when you have eaten and are full and have built good houses and lived in them, and when your herds and flocks multiply and your silver and gold is multiplied and all that you have is multiplied, then your heart be lifted up, and you forget the Lord your God, who brought you out of the land of Egypt, out of the house of slavery, who led you through the great and terrifying wilderness, with its fiery serpents and scorpions and thirsty ground where there was no water, who brought you water out of the flinty rock, who fed you in the wilderness with manna that your fathers did not know, that he might humble you and test you, to do you good in the end. Beware lest you say in your heart, "My power and the might of my hand have gotten me this wealth." You shall remember the Lord your God, for it is he who gives you power to get wealth, that he may confirm his covenant that he swore to your fathers, as it is this day. And if you forget the Lord your God and go after other gods and serve them and worship them, I solemnly warn you today that you shall surely perish. (Deuteronomy 8:11–19)

Moses's words remain a critical warning for us today. Do not forget the Lord when life gets good. Do not become full and ask, "Who is the Lord?" Is this your question? Have you forgotten what the Lord has done for you? Let me refresh your memory.

The Lord is the source of every good and perfect gift.

The Lord is the one who gives life and breath and all things.

The Lord is the one in whom we live and move and have our being.

The Lord is the one who causes our cup to run over.

The Lord is the one who has blessed you with every spiritual blessing in the heavenly places in Christ.

The Lord is the one who supplies all of our needs according to his glorious riches in Jesus Christ our Lord.

The Lord is He who gives us all things freely to enjoy.[4]

LESSON 7: ASK GOD TO GIVE YOU THE RIGHT ATTITUDE ABOUT POVERTY, SO YOU WILL NOT DEFAME HIS NAME

Having too much money can be dangerous. But so can having too little. Not having enough to meet your needs may result in you stealing from others. It is wrong to take what does not belong to you (Exodus 20:15). Stealing is immoral, unethical, and antisocial behavior. I am sure Agur wanted to avoid this. But Agur's primary concern was the spiritual issue that stealing would create with God. In verse 9, Agur explains why he prays against poverty: "lest I be poor and steal and profane the name of my God."

To pray this way reveals that Agur had a healthy respect for the rights of others and a healthy fear of the consequences of unlawful behavior. Ultimately, Agur's prayer reveals a high view of God. Agur did not want to become poor and resort to stealing and in so doing profane the name of God.

Agur did not believe in situational ethics. Do you? You may not know the theory of situational ethics or affirm its principles. But do you practice its lifestyle? Many do unwittingly. We even defend it when we apologize for what we do or do not do by saying, "I have to eat. I have to pay my bills. I have to take care of my responsibilities." Or, my favorite, "I have to do what I have to do!" And so we flex the rules according to the situation. We talk this way as if the meeting of our needs trumps every other responsibility in our lives—even our responsibility to God. And when we think this way, we begin to compromise, negotiate, and hustle to get our needs met.

Such attitudes and action say to the world that God cannot be trusted to take care of us. This profanes the name of God. Romans 8:32 says, "He who did not spare his own Son but gave him up for us all, how will he not also with him graciously give us all things?" Did you get that? If you can trust God to save your soul, you can trust God to take care of you while you are on your way from earth to glory.

Trust God to give you daily bread.

Trust God to meet your needs.

Trust God to provide for you.

Trust God to show you favor.

Trust God to open doors of opportunity.

God will take care of you if you trust in Him.

The cities of Sodom and Gomorrah were taken captive along with several other cities (Genesis 14). Abraham's nephew Lot was among the many captives. So Abraham rounded up several hundred of his servants and went to war against the conquering nations. And he prevailed. Afterward, the king of Sodom offered to split the spoils of war with Abraham. But Abraham refused. He had won the battle but would not enjoy the benefits of victory. Abraham did not abstain because he didn't want to be wealthy. He already was. (He would grow even wealthier in time.) He didn't want to add wealth this way and have the nations say that he became wealthy by taking their stuff. Abraham did not want to receive any wealth that the Lord would not get the credit for. So he refused, because Abraham knew that you can't do God's will your way. The only true blessings are those that result in the glory of God. We should be like Abraham in this regard.

We should also pray like Agur. Forsake falsehood and lies. Don't fall in love with money. Trust God to provide the food that is necessary for you. Wait on the Lord. Expect God to use your weakness as a platform to put His strength on display. And don't forget to give credit where credit is due.

CHAPTER 5

The Kind of Prayer
God Answers

Oh Lord, let your ear be attentive to the prayer of your servant,
and to the prayer of your servants who delight to fear your name,
and give success to your servant today, and grant him mercy
in the sight of this man. Now I was cupbearer to the king.

NEHEMIAH 1:11

The title of this chapter is a back-door acknowledgment that there are some prayers that God will not answer. I repeat: God does not answer every prayer. (See Jeremiah 7:16; Psalm 66:18; 1 Peter 3:7.)

In fact, God will not *listen* to some prayers; much less answer them. This is why the prayer recorded in Nehemiah 1:5–11 is such a helpful example for us.

Nehemiah was preoccupied with God's tendency to ignore certain prayers. "Let your ear be attentive and your eyes open, to hear the prayer of your servant," he prayed (v. 6a). Near the end of his prayer he urged God, "O Lord, let your ear be attentive to the prayer of your servant" (v. 11a). Of course, God has no ears; his statements are called *anthropomorphisms*. They express divine reality in physical terms. God is a spirit (John 4:24) and does not have eyes and ears. Yet Nehemiah ascribes these physical features to God to make a graphic statement of how displeased God is with some prayers.

Think about it. God finds some prayers so unacceptable that He plugs His ears so that He cannot hear and covers His eyes so that He cannot see. But that did not happen to Nehemiah. God heard and answered Nehemiah's prayer. And this God-breathed transcript of Nehemiah's prayer teaches us the kind of prayer God answers.

Now, let me be clear about something before we go any further with this discussion of answered prayer. Do not expect this chapter to give you an easy formula for answered prayer. I hate religious formulas. They domesticate biblical truth, trivialize God's sovereign ways, and rob the walk of faith of its intended sense of adventure. So don't expect any shortcuts to answered prayer here. I plan to give you the long, scenic route to answered prayer.

> **God is not moved by wordy eloquence, vain repetition, emotional intensity, high volume . . . or any other religious hocus-pocus.**

Here it is: God typically answers prayer that is offered by a person who is totally committed to Him. Answered prayer is the natural overflow of a committed life. The life of the one praying is more important to God than the words of the prayer. Why did God answer Nehemiah's prayer? Nehemiah's prayer did not move the hand of God because he said the right words the right way. God accepted Nehemiah's prayer because God accepted Nehemiah. It was not what was being said as much as it was who was talking.

James 5:16b puts it this way: "The prayer of a righteous person has great power as it is working." Translation: God is not moved by wordy eloquence, vain repetition, emotional intensity, high volume, name-it-and-claim-it, or any other religious hocus-pocus. But when a person whose heart is right prays, God's ears are open, God's eyes are attentive, and God's hands are outstretched to answer their prayer.

The question is: What must I do to get God's attention in prayer? How should I pray to win God's approval? Is there a way to pray that moves God to act? I don't know about you, but when I pray, I don't want God to cover His eyes or close His ears. I want God to take off His cosmic headphones, as it were, silence the angels, lean over the balcony of heaven in full attention, and begin reaching for His divine resources to answer my prayer. The prayer of Nehemiah teaches of several important aspects of the kind of prayer God answers.

GOD ANSWERS SINCERE PRAYER

The book of Nehemiah opens in Susa, the winter residence of King Artaxerxes of Persia. Nehemiah was there to fulfill his official duties as the royal cupbearer. One day, Nehemiah's brother, Hanani, showed up with several others from Judah for a visit. I imagine it was a joyful reunion, a warm fellowship. But the mood changed when Nehemiah asked about the condition of the remnant of Jews who had returned to Jerusalem after the Babylonian Captivity. The answer Nehemiah received was bad news. The remnant that had survived the exile was in great trouble and shame. Even worse, the city wall was broken down and its gates destroyed by fire.

When Nehemiah heard this sad report, he sat down and wept and mourned for many days. He was inconsolable. We can't imagine what it was like for Nehemiah to hear that his homeland was demolished. His countrymen were living in a barren land that was once a great city. It was natural for Nehemiah to grieve. For the record, there is nothing spiritual about acting as if life does not hurt when life hurts. The Word of God tells us about many godly men, including Abraham, Moses, David, Jeremiah, and Paul, who wept and mourned. For that matter, Isaiah predicted Jesus would be "a man of sorrows, and acquainted with grief" (Isaiah 53:3). And John reports that Jesus wept (John 11:35).

Be clear: Christians are not instructed not to grieve in the face of life tragedies. We are exhorted not to sorrow as those who have no hope (1 Thessalonians 4:13). Nehemiah sorrowed at the bad news he received about the Jews who had returned to Jerusalem. But he had hope. As Nehemiah wept and mourned, he also fasted and prayed.

Nehemiah prayed. And he prayed sincerely. The sincerity of his prayer is evident by its content (Nehemiah 1:5–11). But the fact that Nehemiah prayed sincerely is also seen in when he prayed, not just what he prayed. He prayed immediately. Nehemiah did not get advice, make a plan, and take action before he took the matter to the Lord. Before he did anything else, Nehemiah prayed about it. That's the kind of prayer God answers. God answers those who make prayer their first response, not their last resort.

Now, don't get me wrong. Nehemiah was definitely a man of action. I would eagerly recommend the book of Nehemiah as a masterful manual on effective leadership, wise planning, shrewd organization, focused activity, and unwavering diligence. But Nehemiah did not make a move without prayer. Read the book of Nehemiah for yourself. You will see that Nehemiah handled everything with prayer. That's sincere prayer. Sincere prayer recognizes that there is much that can be done after you pray, but there is not much that you can do to help the situation until you pray. Sincere prayer recognizes that when we work, we work. But when we pray, God works. Sincere prayer recognizes that it happens after prayer.

I become troubled when I hear someone say, "If you've tried everything, and everything has failed, try God!" I know the person means well. And I understand the sentiment behind the statement. But, in reality, this is just a call to religious hypocrisy. If you only go to God

> **Nehemiah prayed sincerely and he prayed immediately.**

after you have tried everything else, your prayers will inevitably lack one of the most important things God is looking for in prayer: childlike dependence. God is ready, willing, and able to help those who trust in Him. But God is dishonored when we treat Him as a heavenly 9-1-1. Think about it. *I'll call Him when there's an emergency,* you tell yourself. *Maybe He can help with the big things. I* can handle the everyday stuff. But Peter tells us that when it comes to difficulties, you should be "casting *all* your anxieties on him, because he cares for you" (1 Peter 5:7, emphasis added).

One day, a pastor visited a troubled member. She faced many afflictions and was greatly discouraged. When the sister had unburdened herself to her pastor, she pleaded, "Brother Hoffman, what shall I do? What shall I do?" The pastor didn't really know what to say to her. To buy himself a few moments, he read some Scripture. Then he gave her the practical advice he could offer. "You cannot do better than to take *all* of your sorrows to Jesus," he said. "You must tell Jesus." Surprisingly, this off-the-cuff pastoral advice worked! The woman thought about it. She became focused on meditation. Then her countenance changed. And with great joy, she agreed with her pastor, "Yes, I must tell Jesus."

The pastor, Elisha A. Hoffman, soon returned to his study. But he couldn't get that sister's face out of his mind. Her words continued to ring in his ear, "I must tell Jesus. I must tell Jesus. I must tell Jesus." By the time Hoffman reached his study, he had crafted the words to his beloved hymn that Christians continue to sing more than a hundred years later.

> I must tell Jesus all of my trials,
> I cannot bear these burdens alone.
> In my distress He kindly will help me,
> He ever loves and cares for his own.[1]

No matter the prayer—a big emergency or everyday concern—remember that sincere prayer means we have faith in and dependence on God. James gives this important qualification for sincere prayer: "But let [one] ask in faith, with no doubting, for the one who doubts is like a wave of the sea that is driven and tossed by the wind. For that person must not suppose that he will receive anything from the Lord; he is a double-minded man, unstable in all his ways" (James 1:6–8).

GOD ANSWERS REVERENT PRAYER

When Nehemiah heard the bad news about the remnant of Jews who had returned to Jerusalem and the pitiful condition of the city, he immediately took the matter to the Lord in prayer. His prayer began with an invocation: "O Lord God of heaven, the great and awesome God who keeps covenant and steadfast love with those who love him and keep his commandments, let your ear be attentive and your eyes open, to hear the prayer of your servant that I now pray before you day and night for the people of Israel your servants" (Nehemiah 1:5–6).

Nehemiah went to the Lord with a heavy burden. His heart was so troubled that he sat on the floor weeping and mourning for many days. Yet Nehemiah did not rush into God's presence making requests, petitions, and supplications. In fact, Nehemiah does not mention the issue that led him to pray until the very end of the prayer (Nehemiah 1:11). Instead, Nehemiah began his prayer with words of worship, adoration, and praise.

He recognized the transcendence of God: "O Lord God of heaven."

He ascribed majesty to God: "The great and awesome God."

He honored the faithfulness of God: "who keeps covenant and steadfast love with those who love him and keep his commandments."

God answers prayer that is reverent, worshipful, God-intoxicated.

This is the kind of prayer God answers. God answers prayer that is reverent, worshipful, God-intoxicated.

When I began high school, I discovered a new phenomenon. I had classmates who called their parents by their first names. This was totally new to me. I was shocked. But I thought it was kind of cool, at the same time. My classmates seemed "grown up" to me, referring to their dad as "Bill" or the mom as "Jackie."

So I tried it. I went home and started calling my dad, H. B. (My dad only had initials for his name. He did it to me. And I did it to my son.) My dad did not say anything about it. So I continued to do it for several days. I was now cool and grown up too, I thought. Finally, my mom told me how much I was hurting my dad. He thought I was being intentionally disrespectful. And he felt that by calling him H. B., not father, I was rejecting his paternal authority over my life.

That day changed my life. It wiped out my foolish ideas about adulthood. I understood that day that becoming mature did not put me on my father's level. No matter how old I get, there would always be distance between us. My father was not one of my friends. He was my father. And he deserved my respect. Yet it saddens me to admit that the lesson I learned that day about my earthly father is a lesson I am still learning about my heavenly Father.

Unfortunately, this is a common problem among the children of God. We are prone to become nonchalant about the Father in heaven. We suffer from a low view of God. We do not recognize God's sovereign authority over our lives, as we should. And this lack of reverence is often demonstrated in how we pray. Could this be a reason why we do not see more answers to our prayers? Do your prayers lack a proper sense of reverence toward the heavenly Father? Do you know who you are talking to when you pray?

It was God who unrolled the blueprint for the foundation of the world before history's dawning.

It was God who called cosmos out of chaos with his own voice, declaring, "Let there be light."

It was God who sent the earth spinning on its axis, and placed Mother Nature and Father Time on it and commanded them to dance together without getting dizzy.

It was God who made the sun from the brilliance of His own face.

> **God flung the stars, like a million flaming skyrockets against the ebony dome of evening. . . . Do you know who you are talking to when you pray?**

It was God who flung the stars, like a million flaming skyrockets against the ebony dome of evening.

It was God who flung the fleecy white clouds against the azure colored canvas of the vaulted blue.

It was God who gave the lion its roar, the cow its moo, the duck its quack, and the dog its bark.

It was God who took a lump of clay and stamped His image on man's brow. Put the quest for truth in man's heart. Then He exhaled. And man stood on tiptoe as a living being.

It was God who robed Himself in flesh, lived as a blue-collar worker from an ancient ghetto called Nazareth, to bear our sins on the cross.

Do you know who you are talking to when you pray?

Listen, when you don't begin your prayers the way Nehemiah did, you will not be able to conclude your prayers the way Nehemiah did. Nehemiah closed this prayer with a powerful request: "And give success to your servant today, and grant him mercy in the sight of this man" (Nehemiah 1:11). Nehemiah prayed this as the cupbearer of the king. The king was Artaxerxes (Nehemiah 2:1), whose Persian Empire was the world's sole superpower at the time. Artaxerxes was the most powerful man on the face of the earth. There was no higher human being Nehemiah could appeal to. But Nehemiah did not refer to him as the great, mighty, and sovereign Artaxerxes. He didn't even refer to him as the king. Nehemiah just called him "this man." To Nehemiah, Artaxerxes was just another man. Nehemiah could think and talk this way about Artaxerxes, because he first magnified the greatness and glory and goodness of the Lord God in prayer.

Before you tell God about how big your problem is, tell God how big He is! Exalt the Lord in prayer.

Try it. Before you tell God about how big your problem is, tell God how big He is! Exalt the Lord in prayer. Worship him. Reverence the true and living God. Then watch your view of your circumstances change. The greater God becomes to you, the smaller your problems will become. As a pastor, I sometimes have members give me their excuses for why they are absent from corporate worship on the Lord's Day. "With all that I'm dealing with, I'm sure God understands," they claim. He may. But I don't. Knowing what they are going through, I cannot understand why they have not made worship their top priority. God is worthy of our worship, no matter what is going on in our lives. Likewise, when trouble comes, you need to sing and pray and receive the Word to be reminded that God is God.

Your mate is not God. God is God.

Your children are not God. God is God.

Your boss is not God. God is God.

Your teachers and classmates are not God. God is God.

GOD ANSWERS HONEST PRAYER

After offering words of adoration, Nehemiah continued to delay making the primary request that had moved him to pray. He moved from worship to confession of sin instead. His reverence for God led him to deal with the things that were standing between him and God. Nehemiah confessed that the children of Israel had sinned. His family had sinned. And he himself had sinned. "We have acted very corruptly against you," he confessed (v. 7). Both Nehemiah and his people had failed to keep the commandments, statutes, and ordinances of God in the Law of Moses.

Then Nehemiah acknowledged that the reproach of the people and the destruction of the city were only what they deserved. "Remember the word that you commanded your servant Moses, saying, 'If you are unfaithful, I will scatter you among the peoples,'" he prayed (v. 8). The sinfulness of Israel was great, pervasive, and indefensible. And God had given them what they deserved. By the way, be careful of complaining that you deserve something better than what you are experiencing. Believe me, you don't want God to give you what you really deserve.

You would think Nehemiah's confession of sin would have caused God to ignore his prayer. To the contrary, Nehemiah's confession actually motivated God to respond favorably to his prayer. This is the kind of prayer God answers. God answers honest prayer.

King David was honest before God about his sins and their consequence. "For when I kept silent, my bones wasted away through my groaning all day long. For day and night your hand was heavy upon me; my strength was dried up as by the heat of summer. I acknowledged my sin to you, and I did not cover my iniquity. I said, 'I will confess my transgressions to the Lord,' and you forgave the iniquity of my sin" (Psalm 32:3–5).

The Scriptures tell us the outcome of honest confession of our sins:

Whoever conceals his transgressions will not prosper, but he who confesses and forsakes them will obtain mercy. (Proverbs 28:13)

If we confess our sins, he is faithful and just to forgive us our sins and to cleanse us from all unrighteousness. (1 John 1:9)

Unfortunately, confession is a grossly neglected area of prayer, both private prayer and corporate prayer. We are not honest with

God about the sin in our lives. So our prayers go unanswered. The psalmist puts it bluntly: "If I had cherished iniquity in my heart, the Lord would not have listened" (Psalm 66:18). Yet we go on lying to God about who we really are. We lie to people in our lives. We even lie to ourselves. We lie about our real selves because we fail to interpret God through the perfect revelation of Himself in the Lord Jesus Christ. When we fail to view God through the lens of love provided in Christ Jesus, we inevitably try to earn God's favor through our own efforts to be good. And it's impossible to be honest with God when you are trying to impress him with how good you are. So we become hypocrites. And this hypocrisy then flows into all of our relationships.

Consequently, honesty with others and with self is a precious commodity seldom found in either the world or the church. We fear that if we bare our souls, we will be abandoned by friends and ridiculed by our enemies. We all wrestle with the questions raised by Brennan Manning,

> Is there anyone I can level with? Anyone I dare tell that I am benevolent and malevolent, chaste and randy, compassionate and vindictive; selfless and selfish, that beneath my brave words lives a frightened child, that I dabble in religion and pornography, that I have blackened a friend's character, betrayed a trust, violated a confidence, that I am tolerant and thoughtful, a bigot and a blowhard, that I hate hard rock music?[2]

The good news for us ragamuffins is that there is someone we can trust with all of our sins, weaknesses, and limitations. And you'll never believe who that person is! It's the same one we keep running from because of His holiness, justice, and wrath. How can that be? Because He is holy and we are rebels who break His law.

Listen again to Nehemiah's prayer. He recalls God's warning to Israel: "If you are unfaithful, I will scatter you among the nations" (v. 8). This is exactly what God did in the Babylonian captivity. But that is not all the Lord said. He not only issued a warning, He also made a promise: "but if you return to me and keep my commandments and do them, though your outcasts are in the uttermost parts of heaven, from there I will gather them and bring them to the place that I have chosen, to make my name dwell there" (v. 9).

God will not only forgive you, He'll also restore you. . . . It doesn't matter what you have done.

God is holy. In His holiness God says to sinners, "If you turn away from Me, I'll punish you." Yet God is love. In His love God says to sinners, "But if you return to Me, I'll pardon you." Isn't this good news? God is willing to give rebels another chance.

God will not only forgive you, He'll also restore you. He says that even if you are cast out to the farthest part of the heavens, He will get you. He will bring you back. It doesn't matter what you have done. It doesn't matter how long you've been doing it. It doesn't matter how far you have gone. God is waiting for you to trust Him enough to be honest so that He may restore you by His grace.

I read a story about a man who was driving along the New Jersey Turnpike one summer afternoon. A Lincoln Town Car was about a hundred yards ahead of him in the same lane. Suddenly the man saw the right rear door of the Lincoln, still moving at full speed, swing open. Then the passenger threw a collie out of the car, as the car kept going! The dog hit the concrete and rolled into a ditch. But, bleeding profusely, the collie got up and started running after the car and the owner that had cruelly abandoned him. His relentless faithfulness was not conditioned or diminished by the abuse and callous disregard of his master.

But this collie's willingness to pursue the one who spurned him is nothing in comparison to the stubborn love of God. We keep kicking God to the curb. Worse, we hung Him on the cross. Though we did this to the lover of our soul, this "hound of heaven" keeps pursuing us with His furious love. (See the magnificent poem "The Hound of Heaven," by Francis Thompson, for a description of His pursuit of us—who urges us to "rise, clasp My hand, and come!"[3])

Why? Why does God continue to love us? Why has God not just wiped us out once and for all? Why does God keep extending to us another chance? Nehemiah answers: "They are your servants and your people, whom you have redeemed by your great power and your strong hand" (1:10). Nehemiah says, "Lord, the people are no good. But they're Yours! You redeemed them by Your great power and outstretched hand." I love that. Family and friends may reject you if you fail to live up to their standards along the way. But before the journey ever begins with God, He says, "Now, I know you're going to miss the mark. I know you are going to fall short. And I know that you are going to turn away from me at some point. But I want you to know that, whatever happens, I won't change my mind about you. You're still mine." Jeremiah rightly sings, "The steadfast love of the Lord never ceases; his mercies never come to an end; they are new every morning; great is your faithfulness" (Lamentations 3:22–23).

GOD ANSWERS BELIEVING PRAYER

When Nehemiah heard about the conditions of Jerusalem's walls and gates, he made himself available to God to do something about the situation. He was even willing to leave his white-collar job as a royal executive to go rebuild the walls of Jerusalem. Yet nothing would be accomplished in his own strength, wisdom, and authority. No matter how willing Nehemiah was, the success of the entire project rested in the sovereign hands of God. Nehemiah knew that the outcome was in God's hands. So he prayed bold, specific, and courageous prayers: "Give success to your servant today, and grant him mercy in the sight of this man" (v. 11). This is a big, audacious prayer. I know that it may not seem that way on the surface. But the last sentence of verse 11 shows us the magnitude of these requests: "For I was the king's cupbearer" (NKJV).

The ancient Near East was definitely not the land of the free and the home of the brave. Political leaders did not transfer power by any democratic process. Kings ruled with absolute power. If someone desired to be king, the only way was to assassinate the current king. Knowing this, these kings would each assign a cupbearer. The role of the cupbearer is just like it sounds. He carries the king's cup. He is the official food and wine taster. The king would be offered a drink. The cupbearer would taste it first. If the taster doesn't die, the king will take a drink.

As you can imagine, the cupbearer was a trusted position. Eventually the cupbearer became the most important cabinet position in a kingdom. The king trusted the cupbearer with his life. So Nehemiah couldn't just go into the throne room and tell Artaxerxes that he was taking an indefinite leave of absence. He would have never made it out of the room alive! To ask the king to leave his assignment was dangerous.

Moreover, the reason Nehemiah wanted to leave was even more dangerous. Convinced that Jerusalem was filled with political troublemakers, the king had previously ordered that Jerusalem not be rebuilt (Ezra 4).

This was an impossible mission. Nehemiah planned to go to this paranoid king and ask his permission to rebuild a banned city. He would also need to ask for the resources needed to rebuild it, as well as troops to protect him in the process! All of the odds were against him.

But Nehemiah knew a King who is greater than Artaxerxes. And Nehemiah talked to that greater King before he talked to Artaxerxes. He asked the Lord to make him successful and to grant him mercy in the sight of this man. He prayed that the Lord would touch the heart of Artaxerxes, so that he would receive all he needed to get the Lord's work done.

Nehemiah tried something so great for God that he was sure to fail if the Lord didn't help him. That's the kind of prayer God answers.

God answered Nehemiah's prayer. Artaxerxes granted Nehemiah permission to return to his homeland to rebuild the walls that were broken down (Nehemiah 2:6). The king also assigned a royal guard to accompany Nehemiah, lest any danger befall him (Nehemiah 2:7, 9). Artaxerxes even sent Nehemiah with a voucher to get the wood he would need to build the wall, along with enough wood to build Nehemiah a house to live in during his stay (Nehemiah 2:8).

God honored Nehemiah's prayer in such a great way because Nehemiah had great faith in God. He walked by faith and not by sight. He tried something so great for God that he was sure to fail if the Lord didn't help him. That's the kind of prayer God answers. God answers believing prayer.

Well, what is it that you need God to do in your life? Whatever it is, I have great news for you: God is able!

God is able to put your marriage back together.

God is able to bring your wandering child back home.

God is able to heal your sick and hurting body.

God is able to straighten out your finances.

God is able to save your loved ones.

God is able to break that sinful habit you struggle with.

God is able to fulfill every holy desire you have and accomplish every deed prompted by your faith.

The issue is not God's ability to move in the situation. The issue is whether you really believe that God is "able to do exceedingly abundantly above all that [you] ask or think" (Ephesians 3:20 NKJV). Are you willing to step out on faith? Jeremiah 33:3 says, "Call to Me, and I will answer you, and show you great and mighty things, which you do not know" (NKJV). Matthew 7:7 says, "Ask, and it will be given to you; seek, and you will find; knock, and it will be opened to you." And 1 John 5:14 says, "This is the confidence that we have toward him, that if we ask anything according to his will, he hears us." God is able to answer your prayers. Pray sincerely. Pray reverently. Pray honestly. Pray expectantly. Then step back and watch God work!

CHAPTER 6

Can You Handle an
Answered Prayer?

And the king granted me what I asked,
for the good hand of my God was upon me.

NEHEMIAH 2:8

There's much material available to help Christians deal with the mystery of unanswered prayer. Yet unanswered prayer remains a mystery for many of us.

You may be carrying scars from the painful experience of not getting what you prayed for. You called on the Lord, but you did not receive what you asked for. What you sought was not found. The door you knocked on never opened. And you now find yourself struggling with "the mystery of unanswered prayer."

Does God really answer prayer? you ask yourself. Yes, God answers prayer. In fact, answered prayer is the true mystery. Why would God be so good and wise and faithful to answer our prayers? But often we do not know what we are asking for. We do not know the consequences of the things for which we ask. We do not know what it will actually cost us for God to answer our prayers. Yet God knows all and controls all. And He answers according to what will be for our good and His glory.

I know how you feel when a prayer seems to be unanswered. Yet the puzzle of why God does not answer certain prayers is easily solved when you consider the puzzle of why God chooses to answer any prayers at all.

Mark it down: The Lord God does not owe you anything. That is, God does not rightfully owe you anything except divine judgment, holy wrath, and eternal condemnation. Yet God the Father commands us to come to Him in prayer. And He waits with open arms to hear and answer and work on behalf of His children. And because of this divine favor upon every believer, we should never allow unanswered prayer to cause us to question the power, wisdom, or goodness of God in our lives. Instead, we can live in confidence that God will hear and answer our prayers. The problem is that we often miss or mishandle the answers God gives, because we are not ready to receive the things we ask God for.

Have you ever thought about that? Have you ever wrestled with the fact that answered prayer can put your life in jeopardy?

Have you ever considered the fact that it could be more dangerous and detrimental to your well-being for God to give you some of the things you want, rather than withholding them?

Ask King Hezekiah about the danger of prayer answered with a yes. One day, the prophet Isaiah visits Hezekiah with a message from God. Hezekiah is deathly sick. But the prophet does not come with good news. His is a message of impending doom: "Thus says the Lord, 'Set your house in order, for you shall die; you shall not recover'" (2 Kings 20:1). But Hezekiah will not accept this message as the final word. He turns his face to the wall and prays to the Lord. Do you know what happens? God answers Hezekiah's prayer with a yes.

Before Isaiah can make it off the palace grounds, God commands him to go back to Hezekiah. There is an updated message. The Lord will raise him from his sick bed in three days and add fifteen years to his life (vv. 4–6).

It is a miracle of answered prayer. But the end of that same chapter records how this miracle feeds Hezekiah's pride, as the king displays all his wealth to visitors from Babylon (vv. 12–13). So God judges Hezekiah, promising that the Babylonians would overthrow his kingdom. The opening verse of the very next chapter reports that during those fifteen additional years, Hezekiah has a son named Manasseh. Second Kings 21:2 reports that Manasseh "did what was evil in the sight of the Lord." I wonder if Hezekiah ever wished he had died when Isaiah showed up with the fatal diagnosis.

Consider another example of the trouble a positive answer to prayer can bring. The children of Israel demand a king (1 Samuel 8). Reluctantly, and with great disappointment, Samuel the prophet prays that God would give them a king. His prayer is answered. The people will receive what they desired. But the Lord commands Samuel to warn the people that the king will send their sons to war, make some of them slaves, and steal the proceeds from their hard work (vv. 11–17). When that happens, the prophet says, "you will cry out because of your king, whom you have chosen for yourselves, but the Lord will not answer you." But the people refuse to obey Samuel's warning. And they say, "No! But there shall be a king over us." God gives Israel what they want. And the rest is history.

Here's one more example. One day the mother of James and John asks Jesus to give her sons the chief seats of honor in the kingdom—one on His left hand and one on His right. The request is definitely a statement of faith. This mother believes Jesus is the King and that His kingdom will come. But her request is tainted with sinful ambition.

We tend to focus on the times when God says no and ignore the times when God says grow.

Jesus responds, "You do not know what you are asking. Are you able to drink the cup that I am to drink?" (Matthew 20:22). I believe the Lord often responds to our prayers the same way He responded to the request of James and John's mother: "You do not know what you ask."

There is an often used little outline that describes how God typically answers prayer.

If the request is wrong, God says no.

If the timing is wrong, God says slow.

If you are wrong, God says grow.

But if the request is right, the timing is right, and you are right, God says go.

Our tendency is to focus on the times when God says no and ignore the times when God says grow. But I warn you that it is dangerous for God to put something in your hand without first doing something to your heart to get you ready for what He puts in your hands.

So let me ask you a pertinent question about your prayer life: Can you handle an answered prayer? I raise this question in light of what Nehemiah experienced after he prayed for divine intervention that he go rebuild the walls of Jerusalem. The very next passage (Nehemiah 2:1–10) shows us three marks of a person who can handle an answered prayer.

THE DISCIPLINE OF WAITING ON GOD

One day, as Nehemiah serves the king at Artaxerxes' winter residence, Nehemiah's brother Hanani shows up with some guys from Judah. During their visit, Nehemiah asks about the condition of the Jews who had returned to Jerusalem after the Babylonian captivity. He also asks about the condition of the city itself. The answer he receives is filled with bad news. The people are in great distress and reproach. The city walls are broken down, their gates fallen by fire.

"As soon as I heard these words I sat down and wept and mourned for days," Nehemiah testifies, "and I continued fasting and praying before the God of heaven" (1:4). Nehemiah 1:5–11 records Nehemiah's prayer, in which he asks God for the opportunity to go to Jerusalem and rebuild the city

The book of Nehemiah begins in the Hebrew month Chislev,

mid-November to mid-December on our calendar (v. 1). But when God answers Nehemiah's prayer in the next chapter, it is now the month of Nisan, mid-March to mid-April on our calendar (2:1). Four months have passed between chapter 1 when Nehemiah takes his situation to God in prayer and chapter 2 when God obviously acts in response to Nehemiah's prayers.

In the beginning of chapter 2, Nehemiah continues to fulfill his duties as the king's cupbearer. But he has not forgotten or ignored the issues he had taken to God in prayer. In fact, he is still so troubled by the news he received over four months ago that he does something that is totally uncharacteristic of him (and unwise for any cupbearer). He expresses sadness in the presence of the king. No one in the royal court displays sadness in the presence of the king. The king may take it that you are up to something. So Nehemiah had always kept his cool.

Only this day does his sorrow reveal itself, and the king notices Nehemiah's sad countenance. He asks Nehemiah why he is so sad. Was he sick? Had someone died? What was going on with Nehemiah? The significant point to get out of the king's question about Nehemiah's sorrow is that the king has to ask. Nehemiah had carried a heavy burden for months. But he had never uttered a word about it to Artaxerxes. He just went about his daily routine as if nothing were wrong. This is the first mark of a person who can handle an answered prayer. It is the discipline of waiting on God's perfect timing. Yet today Nehemiah lapses into sadness.

Do you know how the Chinese bamboo tree grows? The seed is planted. It is watered and fertilized. But nothing happens the first year. During the second year, the seed is watered and fertilized. Still nothing happens. The same thing happens the third and fourth years. Nothing. But during the fifth year of watering and fertilizing, the Chinese bamboo trees grows roughly ninety feet in approximately six weeks. Does the tree grow ninety feet in six weeks or five years? It actually takes five years for it to grow ninety feet. You may not see any growth during the first four years. But without watering and fertilizing the seed each year, there would never be the sudden growing during that short period.

> **Be sure you do not run ahead of the Lord. Do not follow the foolish advice that says, "Don't just stand there. Do something."**

All of us have "bamboo" experiences in life. And many of us never grow into what God designed us to be because we erroneously think that yes means now. We keep missing our appointment with answered prayer, because we have not learned to stay in God's waiting room until He tells us to move. To be in the will of God is to do the right thing the right way for the right reason and at the right time. So you can step outside of God's will, even though your goals, plans, and motives are right. You must make sure that you do not run ahead of the Lord. Do not follow the foolish advice that says, "Don't just stand there. Do something." Until you get clear direction from the Lord, this is heaven's agenda for you: Don't just do something. Stand there.

At the Red Sea, Moses said to the children of Israel, "Fear not, stand firm, and see the salvation of the Lord, which he will work for you today" (Exodus 14:13).

Naomi advised her daughter-in-law Ruth, "Wait, my daughter, until you learn how the matter turns out, for the man will not rest but will settle the matter today" (Ruth 3:18).

The Lord God commands, "Be still, and know that I am God" (Psalm 46:10).

That is exactly what Nehemiah does. When he receives the bad news about Judah, he takes his burden to the Lord. And when he gives it to the Lord, he takes his hands off it. Nehemiah does not march into the king's quarters and demand a leave of absence to go rebuild Jerusalem. That would have gotten him killed. He does not call a meeting of like-minded people to share his plans with and listen to their ideas. That would have gotten him discouraged. And he does not make any thoughtless, emotional, and rash decisions. That would have gotten him nowhere. When Nehemiah receives the bad news about Judah, he takes his burden to the Lord and leaves it there.

Nehemiah waits on God to answer his prayer. He waits on God to soften the king's heart. He waits on God to open an opportunity for him to move. This is what you must do if you are going to be ready for an answered prayer.

Wait on God to answer.

Wait on God to speak.

Wait on God to respond.

Wait on God to move.

Wait on God to keep His promise.

The psalmist declared, "I waited patiently for the Lord; he inclined to me and heard my cry. He drew me up from the pit of destruction, out of the miry bog, and set my feet upon a rock, making my steps secure. He put a new song in my mouth, a song of praise to our God. Many will see and fear, and put their trust in the Lord" (Psalm 40:1–3). Now read those verses again and note all the things the Lord did for the psalmist simply because he waited for the Lord. The prophet Isaiah assures us, "They who wait for the Lord shall renew their strength; they shall mount up with wings like eagles; they shall run and not be weary; they shall walk and not faint" (40:31). And James counsels, "And let steadfastness have its full effect, that you may be perfect and complete, lacking in nothing" (1:4). Wait on the Lord.

THE DEVOTION OF WATCHING FOR GOD

The fact that Nehemiah was a royal cupbearer tells us that he was an even-tempered man. He had never expressed sadness in the presence of the king. Yet this day, while serving the king and queen in a private banquet, Nehemiah's sorrow within shows itself. Unintentionally, Nehemiah's countenance, attitude, and demeanor begin to change. Artaxerxes notices his cupbearer's expression. "Nehemiah," he responded, "what's the matter with you? You don't look well at all. And I know it's not physical. There's something going on in your heart" (paraphrase of 2:2).

Nehemiah's great sorrow quickly turns into great fear when Artaxerxes confronts him about his attitude. Ancient Near Eastern kings were temperamental men. If the king is everything he believes he is, why would his servants have to be sad? Sad-looking servants inevitably raised royal suspicions. And remember that these ancient kings were so paranoid that they had cupbearers to pre-taste their food and drinks. If that cupbearer started looking strange, it better be because of food poisoning. If not, the king would conclude the cupbearer himself was up to something. And that cupbearer would be banished from the king's presence at best or killed right on the spot at worst.

Nehemiah has every right to be afraid. However, he keeps his cool long enough to notice that Artaxerxes' words and tone express concern rather than anger or suspicion. Nehemiah thinks to himself, *This may be the opening I've been waiting on.* But he isn't sure. So he responds cautiously. "Let the king live forever!" he said. "Why should not my face be sad, when the city, the place of my fathers' graves, lies in ruins, and its gates have been destroyed by fire?" (Nehemiah 2:3).

What a shrewd answer. Ezra 4 reports that the enemies of Judah had convinced the king that Jerusalem was filled with political troublemakers. The king had responded by making a decree that the city was not to be rebuilt. Nehemiah knows this. And wisely, he does not directly mention Judah or Jerusalem. Instead, he appeals to the common ancient eastern respect for the burial place of the dead. And it works. Artaxerxes gives Nehemiah a royal blank check and says: "What are you requesting?" (Nehemiah 2:4a). When Artaxerxes responds so favorably, Nehemiah knows it has to be the Lord. "So I prayed to the God of heaven," he reports (Nehemiah 2:4b).

Nehemiah prays an emergency 9-1-1 prayer. And God answers. God answers Nehemiah's emergency prayer because Nehemiah had spent extended time in prayer before the emergency. He had been praying for four months that God would open an opportunity for him. So when the king does not get angry or suspicious over Nehemiah's open sorrow, his spiritual radar immediately tells him that God is moving. And when he is sure it is God, Nehemiah prays. He doesn't say, "If it pleases the king, give me a few days to fast and pray, then I'll get back to you and tell you what I want." If he had done that, the window of opportunity would have been closed. And it may have never been opened again. So when Artaxerxes

> **God answered Nehemiah's emergency prayer because Nehemiah had spent extended time in prayer before the emergency.**

offers him a blank check, Nehemiah immediately offers a quick prayer to God and says: "Lord, this is it. Please, give me wisdom so that I don't mess this up." This is the second mark of the person who can handle an answered prayer. It is the devotion of watching for God's divine intervention.

When a small country town faced flooding from a nearby river after a torrential rainstorm, city officials told the citizens to evacuate. But the pastor of the local church refused to go. "I've prayed to God for deliverance," he argued. "And I'm going to stay right here and wait on God to deliver me." The authorities didn't question the faith of this man of God. So they left him in the church.

The water kept rising. And the authorities became concerned. They went back to the church to rescue the preacher. But again he refused to go. The Lord was going to deliver him. The next time they came to get him, the water was so high, they had to come in a boat. But again he refused to go. The last time they came to rescue him, the water was so high that the preacher had fled to the roof of the church for safety. Yes, he still refused to go.

Of course, he died in the flood. And when he got to heaven, he was one ticked-off preacher man. "What happened, Lord?" he demanded. "I prayed and asked you to deliver me from the flood. I stood on my faith before a watching world. And I didn't waver, in spite of the circumstances. But you didn't save me. Why, Lord?"

"Son," replied the Lord, "who do you think it was who kept sending those boats after you?"

I submit that you are not ready for an answered prayer if, while you wait on God, you are not also watching for God. You can miss your answer if you are looking in one direction as God is moving in another. It is a matter of focus. Nehemiah was focused on God. Because of his God focus, Nehemiah didn't need an overt miracle, a prophetic word, or a supernatural sign to know that God was at work on his behalf. He heard the voice of God in the words of the king. He saw the hand of God. He felt the leading of God to greater things while at work in the midst of his normal, ordinary, daily routine. And I tell you, if your situation is going to change; you must stop being so preoccupied with the situation. You must put your focus on God.

When your focus is on God, He can lead you. You won't try to lead Him. Stop asking God to bless what you're doing. Start asking God to help you do what He's blessing. Jesus instructs, "But seek first the kingdom of God and his righteousness, and all these things will be added to you" (Matthew 6:33). Solomon counseled his children, "Trust in the Lord with all your heart, and do not lean on your own understanding. In all your ways acknowledge him, and he will make straight your paths" (Proverbs 3:5–6).

The psalmist affirms that God wants to and is able to lead us. "I will instruct you and teach you in the way you should go; I will counsel you with my eye upon you" (Psalm 32:8). Translation: You will never get what you want from God by focusing on what you want to get from God. You must learn to focus on the Lord in every situation. Did you get that?

Don't focus on the need. Focus on God.

Don't focus on the promotion. Focus on God.

Don't focus on the relationship. Focus on God.

Don't focus on the healing. Focus on God.

Don't focus on the blessing. Focus on God.

THE DUTY OF WORKING WITH GOD

Prayer is not an excuse for idleness, slothfulness, or negligence. As I said earlier, answered prayer requires spiritual partnership with God. Without God, you cannot do it. But without you, God will not do it. So if you are going to be ready for an answered prayer, you must learn to wait on God, watch for God, and work with God. There are two ways you can work with God in answer to your prayer. Be ready for the opportunity. And be ready for the opposition.

Get ready for the opportunity. Nehemiah prayed, "Give success to your servant today, and grant him mercy in the sight of this man" (Nehemiah 1:11). Remember, Nehemiah was praying about the wall of Jerusalem that was broken down and burned. But notice how he prayed about it. He did not pray as we sometimes pray. He didn't say, "Lord, the wall of Jerusalem needs rebuilding. I know you are able, Lord. Rebuild the wall, Lord. You can do it, Lord. There is nothing too hard for you, Lord. I praise you in advance for what you are going to do, Lord. Amen."

Many of us pray like that. And that may be why we are not ready for an answered prayer. The problem is not that it is an untrue, insincere, or doubt-filled prayer. The problem is that it is a prayer for divine intervention, rather than a prayer for personal responsibility. I believe Nehemiah was ready for an answered prayer because he did not just pray for a miracle. He prayed for an opportunity. He did not just pray for God to step in and do something. He prayed for God to open the door so that he could step up and do something.

Could that be why your prayers don't work?

Could it be that you are praying for a miracle, rather than an opportunity? Could it be that you have been praying for the Lord to save a friend, but you are not praying that the Lord would help you to be a faithful witness to the person?

Could it be that you have been praying that the Lord would bless your children to grow the right way, but you have not been praying about your own lifestyle, choices, and leadership that directly affect that child's development?

Could it be that you have been praying for a promotion, but you have not been praying for the Lord to help you to be diligent with your present assignment, so that you can prove yourself worthy of that promotion?

The sad fact is that all too often we pray for miracles, rather than opportunities, because we are cheap. A miracle does not cost you anything. You can just sit back and watch God work. But if you pray for an opportunity, you have to get up, make a personal commitment, and make yourself available for God to use you as a part of the answer to your own prayers.

This is how Nehemiah prayed. In fact, Nehemiah was so willing to partner with God that he was getting ready even when he did not see how it was going to happen. When Artaxerxes asked Nehemiah, "What are you requesting?" (2:4), Nehemiah did not respond by saying, "Well, I don't know. We're just going to walk by faith." Or, "I have not thought it through that clearly." Or, "Give me some time to get my ducks in a row." Nehemiah was ready for the opportunity. He was able to specifically ask the king to send him to Jerusalem to rebuild the wall (v. 5). Nehemiah gave the king a time schedule (v. 6). He asked for official letters to provide him safe passage through the various provinces (v. 7). He asked for the supplies he would need to build the wall, the citadel around the temple, and his own house. Nehemiah had so thoroughly worked out his plan that he even knew the name of the guy who ran the king's forest, Asaph. Even when it did not seem there was

Faith is not a substitute for careful planning. People of faith need orderly minds.

any hope that his prayer would be answered, Nehemiah was still getting ready for the Lord to open an opportunity.

Mark it down: Faith is not a synonym for disorder or a substitute for careful planning. People of faith need orderly minds.

"The presence of faith," says Charles Swindoll, "does not mean the absence of organization."

Get ready for the opposition. Not long after I began serving my first pastorate, I was invited to speak out of state. I was still in the "honeymoon" period. Things were going great. And I fully expected that the upward momentum would continue without ceasing. It was all I could talk about. I remember sitting in the restaurant with the pastor, schooling him with my naïve and foolish notions about ministry. When I finished, he said, "H. B., I'm glad the Lord is blessing your honeymoon period at the church. But I want you to know that if you come here next year singing this same song, I'll know that you haven't really done anything there. If you attempt to do anything great for the Lord, things will get worse."

In my youthful ignorance and arrogance, I dismissed his comments. I told myself that he was just a bitter old preacher who couldn't stand to see the Lord blessing a young man! But that was before some of the dear old saints gave me the whipping of my life.

We met for lunch a year later. When I arrived he asked he how things were going. I told him, "It got worse."

This is what happened with Nehemiah.

Many commentators cut off the first part of Nehemiah chapter 2 at verse 8 or 9, excluding verse 10 from this narrative. Admittedly, this verse ends the scene on an anticlimactic note. Up to this point, events have been going Nehemiah's way. He has received the king's permission to go rebuild the walls of Jerusalem. He has received all the resources he needs to get the job done. And he has been assured that he will have a royal guard to accompany him. What more could he ask for?

But then things got worse. "But when Sanballat the Horonite and Tobiah, the Ammonite servant, heard this, it displeased them greatly that someone had come to seek the welfare of the people of Israel" (v. 10). On the surface, it seems anticlimactic to end this scene with the presence of opposition. But the presence of Sanballat and Tobiah really doesn't mess up the story. Such opposition is often essential, because you are not ready for an answered prayer without facing some challenge, problem, or difficulty.

When my father would hear people say that they did not want to make any enemies, he would remind them, "You don't have to make enemies. They come ready-made."

I can hear Nehemiah saying, "Amen."

Sanballat and Tobiah did not even know Nehemiah. All they knew was that Nehemiah was coming to help Jerusalem, and they became deeply disturbed. That's the way the enemy works. Some people who do not like you do not even know you.

Some of us let the slightest offense cause us to forsake the assignment God has given to us. But if you are going to do something, you must be ready for opposition. Mark it down. When you walk by faith, you will invariably collide with a Sanballat and Tobiah. When you decide to arise and build, the enemy decides to arise and disrupt. The apostle Paul wrote, "For a wide door for effective work has opened to me, and there are many adversaries" (1 Corinthians 16:9).

It seems strange to put these two ideas together—an opened door and many adversaries. But that's the way it goes. The good news is that the God who is in control of the opportunity is also in control of our adversaries.

CHAPTER 7

A Godly Attitude toward
Material Possessions

*But who am I, and what is my people, that we should be
able thus to offer willingly? For all things come from you,
and of your own have we given you.*

1 CHRONICLES 29:14

The final, official act of David as king of Israel is recorded in 1
Chronicles 29:10–19, as the king offers a public, joyful, God-
entranced prayer in response to the generosity of Israel.

A sacred box called the ark of the covenant represented the
presence of God to Israel. The ark rested in the tabernacle—a tent
erected as a meeting place for God and Israel. But David's spiritual
devotion deemed it unacceptable that the Lord's holy presence did
not have a permanent dwelling place. He desired to build a temple
for God. But the Lord would not allow David to build a house for

him, because David was a man of war who had shed blood.

The Lord did make several gracious concessions, however. God approved the building of the temple and revealed to David the detailed plans for its construction. Likewise, God chose Solomon, David's son and heir to the throne, to build the temple. Then the Lord graciously allowed David to lead the offering to secure the resources Solomon would need to build the temple.

The people and the leaders responded with generosity. First Chronicles 29:1–9 records the offering given by David, his leaders, and the people of Israel for the temple project. It is estimated that they collected some 375 tons of gold, silver, and precious stones for the temple. It must have been a remarkable scene. The chronicler reports, "Then the people rejoiced because they had given willingly, for with a whole heart they had offered freely to the Lord. David the king also rejoiced greatly" (v. 9).

> David's prayer teaches us a generous hand flows from a godly heart.

In response to this generous offering, David prayed a prayer that is even more remarkable than the offering that prompted it, because it reveals the theological convictions that led to the generous offering. His prayer teaches us a generous hand flows from a godly heart.

One day a mother sent her teenaged son down to the florist to pick up some flowers for the dinner table. He obeyed. But he didn't like it. He did not want his friends to see him. Without a doubt, they would make fun of him and his flowers. But not too long after this, the young man fell in love with a beautiful young lady who stole his heart. And he returned to that same florist's shop to buy a bouquet for the object of his affection. This time, however, he carried the flowers down the street with great pride and joy. The teen did not care who saw him or what they would think and say. He was just thinking of the love of his life and of how happy she would be to get the flowers and how happy he was to be the one to bring them to her.

In the same way, how you manage your money expresses your devotion to God. Jesus said, "Do not lay up for yourselves treasures on earth, where moth and rust destroy and where thieves break in and steal, but lay up for yourselves treasures in heaven, where neither moth nor rust destroys and where thieves do not break in and steal. For where your treasure is, there your heart will be also" (Matthew 6:19–21). You cannot give willingly, regularly, proportionally, sacrificially, and joyfully without a proper perspective on God, yourself, and your material possessions. David's prayer teaches us three godly attitudes toward material possessions.

GOD-EXALTING WORSHIP

In his book *Stewards of God*, Milo Kauffman relates the story of a poor Hindu in Nepal who brought the last of his rice as an offering to his god. A neighbor told him, "You must not do that. You have to live." His answer was, "No, I don't have to live. But I do have to worship."[1]

That was David and Israel's attitude when they were given the opportunity to give to the temple project. This God-centered priority of worship is expressed in the first part of David's prayer, when he "blessed the Lord in the presence of all the assembly" (v. 10). David stood before the assembled nation and blessed the Lord with high praise. If our nation's media covered this event, they would have highlighted David's leadership, his cabinet's example, the people's sacrifice, the economy's strength, and the project's social benefits. But David bypassed the human elements of the generous act and blessed the Lord for the offering. Without denying the willful and wholehearted generosity of the people, David gave God the highest praise and full credit for the offering. David said, "Blessed are you, O Lord, the God of Israel our father, forever and ever."

David declared that good, holy, and wonderful things should be said about God continually and eternally.

Notice that David did not merely bless God for the special events of that particular day. He declared that good, holy, and wonderful things should be said about God continually and eternally. This reminds us of what Jesus taught us about true worship: "But the hour is coming, and is now here, when the true worshipers will worship the Father in spirit and truth, for the Father is seeking such people to worship him. God is spirit, and those who worship him must worship in spirit and truth" (John 4:23–24).

Real worship is in spirit and truth. We ought to bless God for what He has done for us. But we ought to also bless God beyond what He does for us. True worship does not bless God merely because you have received a blessing or because you are trying to get a blessing. True worship blesses God because God is God. It recognizes that no matter what my personal situation may be—good or bad—God is worthy to be praised forever and ever.

In 1 Chronicles 29:11–12, David explains why we should bless the Lord forever:

> Yours, O Lord, is the greatness and the power and the glory and the victory and the majesty, for all that is in the heavens and in the earth is yours. Yours is the kingdom, O Lord, and you are exalted as head above all. Both riches and honor come from you, and you rule over all. In your hand are power and might, and in your hand it is to make great and to give strength to all.

One commentator rightly said of these verses that David "ransacks the theological dictionary" for terms expressing God's infinite worthiness. But let me present this explanation of God's worthiness to you in two simple statements.

God is great. First Chronicles 29:11 tells us that God is great because God is self-sufficient. David says, "Yours, O Lord, is the greatness and the power and the glory and the victory and the majesty, for all that is in the heavens and in the earth is yours." David declared that God is great, powerful, glorious, victorious, and majestic for one simple reason: God owns everything in heaven and on earth. David says it this way in another place: "The earth is the Lord's and the fullness thereof, the world and those who dwell therein" (Psalm 24:1). God is great because everything belongs to Him and He does not need anything from anybody. "If I were hungry, I would not tell you," says the Lord, "for the world and its fullness are mine" (Psalm 50:12). The Lord is self-sufficient. He has everything. He needs nothing.

Verse 11 also tells us that God is great because He is absolutely sovereign. David continues, "Yours is the kingdom, O Lord, and you are exalted as head above all." King David will relinquish his throne to his son, Solomon, shortly (vv. 22–23). But before he does, David acknowledged that the kingdom does not belong to him. And it does not belong to Solomon. The kingdom does not belong to any mortal. It belongs to the Lord, who is the sovereign head of all creation.

> **David acknowledged that the kingdom does not belong to him . . . but to the Lord, the sovereign head of all creation.**

Some scholars believe this statement is the basis of the longer ending of the Lord's Prayer: "Yours is the kingdom and the power and the glory forever" (Matthew 6:13). Regardless, David's prayer tells us that the Lord, who is the self-sufficient owner of everything, freely and fully reigns over all that He owns in absolute sovereignty. God is great because He owns everything and He controls everything.

God is good. David's next statement in this great prayer teaches us that our great God, who owns and controls everything, is also a good God who generously shares His infinite resources. David says, "Both riches and honor come from you, and you rule over all. In your hand are power and might, and in your hand it is to make great and to give strength to all" (1 Chronicles 9:12). In this verse, David addresses several fundamental questions about life that you may be wondering about.

How does a person become rich? David's answer: through God.

How does a person reach a place of honor in his or her life? David's answer: through God.

How does a person become great? David's answer: by God's help.

How does a person become strong? Again, David's answer: with God's help.

God alone is the source of all riches, honor, greatness, and strength. James puts it this way: "Every good gift and every perfect gift is from above, coming down from the Father of lights with whom there is no variation or shadow due to change" (1:17).

That's David's grand declaration: God is great. God is good. How should we respond to these two glorious attributes of God? I'll let my children tell you. The simple mealtime prayer my children offered to God

You should not spend your life complaining about your situation. You ought to thank God for life . . . for grace, mercy, and love.

when they were little models how we ought to respond to our awesome God: "God is great. God is good. Let us thank Him for this food." If you know that God is great and God is good, you should not spend your life fussing, complaining, and whining about your situation. You ought to thank God for life, health, and strength. Thank God for food, clothing, and shelter. Thank God for grace, mercy, and love. Thank God for the death, burial, and resurrection of Jesus Christ.

If you know that God is great and good, you ought to offer joyful praise to God. That was David's conclusion in 1 Chronicles 29:13, as he prays. "And now we thank you, our God, and praise your glorious name."

GOD-CENTERED HUMILITY

David's prayer also teaches us about a second godly attitude toward material possessions—humility. When we receive the gracious gifts of God, but refuse to give generously back to God, it is an expression of sinful pride. Think about it.

In 1 Chronicles 29:14, David contrasts God's infinite greatness and our absolute dependence with a provocative question: "But who am I, and what is my people, that we should be able thus to offer willingly?" I know this is a rhetorical question, but let's answer it anyway. David is nobody. And his people are nothing. David is not expressing low self-esteem when he talks like this. He's expressing high God-esteem. He knew and acted on this humbling truth revealed in his prayer: *Our possessions belong to God.*

There is a sense in which getting your theology of life right is as simple as riding a seesaw. You remember riding a seesaw, don't you? On a seesaw, only one person can be up at a time. If Jack is up, Jill is down. If Jill is up, Jack is down. It is the same way in life. Either God is exalted as you humble yourself. Or God is dishonored and you exalt yourself.

Here's a great truth about humility: Humility is the best friend you have. And the other side of the seesaw: Pride is the worst enemy you have.

David knew his place. He recognized that the generous offering he and his people had given did not put them on God's level. It did not put God into their debt. And it did not make them any more special to God

Jesus instructed His disciples, "So you also, when you have

done all that you were commanded, say, 'We are unworthy servants; we have only done what was our duty'" (Luke 17:10). That is to be our position toward anything we do right. We are unworthy servants. The Lord doesn't owe us anything. We have only done our duty. How much more should this be the case in light of the fact that we have not done all that the Master has commanded us to do.

> **God is the source of everything we possess, receive, and enjoy.**

David asked, "But who am I, and what is my people, that we should be able thus to offer willingly?" Then he clearly stated the point he was trying to make by stating this often forgotten truth: "For all things are from you, and of your own have we given you" (1 Chronicles 29:14). God is the source of everything we possess, receive, and enjoy. David knew *his possessions belong to God.* Paul amplifies that truth in Romans: "For from him and through him and to him are all things. To him be glory forever. Amen" (11:36).

God is the first Cause, the effective Cause, and the final Cause of all things.

God is the Source, the Sustainer, and the Significance of all things.

God is the Source, the Force, and the Course of all things.

God is the Alpha and the Omega (Revelation 21:6; 22:13) and every letter in between!

This is the most fundamental principle of Christian stewardship: God owns it all! God owns everything. We own nothing—not a house, not a car, not a toothbrush. It all belongs to God. Therefore, whenever we give to God, we are only giving back to God what already belongs to Him. So when we begin to think to ourselves, "Do I really have to give that much to God?" we are thinking about the matter all wrong. The truth is that God allows us to keep so much of His money. It all belongs to God.

Furthermore, *our lives are sustained by God*. It is said that the late novelist Alex Haley kept a picture in his office of a turtle sitting on a fence. Inevitably, he would be asked about the meaning of the picture. And he would explain that if you

We are not independent nor self-sufficient people. God sustains our lives.

see a turtle sitting on a fence, you know that it didn't get there by itself. That is a fact of life that we all need to come to grips with. We are not self-made people. We are not independent people. We are not self-sufficient people. God sustains our lives. David confesses this in his prayer: "For we are strangers before you and sojourners, as all our fathers were. Our days on the earth are like a shadow, and there is no abiding" (1 Chronicles 29:15).

In this verse, David makes two statements that affirm the truth that God sustains our lives. First, David says, "We are strangers before you and sojourners, as all our fathers were." David viewed himself and his nation as resident aliens living in a land that was not their own. This is not a statement of alienation from the world around them, for David says that they are strangers and sojourners before God. That is, God did not owe them anything. Likewise, David says, "Our days on the earth are like a shadow, and there is no abiding." This truth about the transience of human life is constantly repeated in Scripture. Job stated, "Man who is born of a woman is few of days and full of trouble. He comes out like a flower and withers; he flees like a shadow and continues not" (Job 14:1–2). Moses prayed, "For all our days pass away under your wrath; we bring our years to an end like a sigh" (Psalm 90:9). And James taught, "Yet you do not know what tomorrow will bring. What is your life? For you are a mist that appears for a little time and then vanishes" (4:14). We are weak creatures of the moment who are sustained by the everlasting Lord of life.

Our generosity is imparted by God. Did you know that your generosity is always the result of divine compulsion? The sad indictment is that we are all stingy people. It's one of the ugly realities of our fallen nature. One of the first words many children learn is "Mine!" That's how we are. We are naturally stingy people. We are naturally acquirers, not donators. We are naturally reservoirs, not rivers. And many of us even consciously and intentionally embrace a philosophy of life that says, "Get all you can, can all you get, and then sit on the can, so you won't have to share it with anybody."

It is only the sovereign grace of God moving on the heart that causes us to give what we have away, rather than hoarding it for ourselves. David affirms this: "O Lord our God, all this abundance that we have provided for building you a house for your holy name comes from your hand and is all your own" (1 Chronicles 29:16).

GOD-HONORING TRUST

Trust that God knows your heart. Toward the end of his prayer, David states a fundamental theological principle that ought to shape how we think and live: "I know, my God, that you test the heart and have pleasure in uprightness" (v. 17).

You can fool people; but you cannot fool God. You can even fool yourself; but you cannot fool God. God knows your heart. The Lord admonished the prophet Samuel, "For the Lord sees not as man sees: man looks on the outward appearance, but the Lord looks on the heart" (1 Samuel 16:7). God knows your heart. And He uses money to test what is in your heart. The Lord is not testing you to discover what's in your heart. He already knows that. He tests us to reveal what is in our heart.

How you spend your money is a true, objective, and independent monitor of where your heart is. And many times the Lord gives us more than what He knows we need as a test to reveal what's in our hearts. Jesus said,

> One who is faithful in a very little is also faithful in much, and one who is dishonest in a very little is also dishonest in much. If then you have not been faithful in the unrighteous wealth, who will entrust to you the true riches? And if you have not been faithful in that which is another's who will give you that which is your own? No servant can serve two masters, for either he will hate the one and love the other, or he will be devoted to the one and despise the other. You cannot serve God and money. (Luke 16:10–13)

I repeat, God knows what's in your heart. And He uses money as a test to reveal what's in your heart. First Chronicles 29:17 tells us what God is looking for in your heart. He takes "pleasure in uprightness." God is pleased when He sees sincerity, purity, authenticity, integrity, and godliness in our hearts. And one of the clearest ways this is evidenced is by what we do with the money that God entrusts to us. If your heart is set on money, not God, He sees. And if your heart is set on God, not money, He sees. David knew this. So he confesses: "In the uprightness of my heart I have freely offered all these things, and now I have seen your people who are present here, offering freely and joyously to you" (v. 17b).

First, David speaks for himself and says that he has given with an upright heart. He has not given with ulterior motives, such as to win the applause of people or receive a blessing from God. Then he speaks for his people. He vouches for their upright hearts, because he has seen them give freely and joyously. An upright heart gives freely and joyously. Paul says, "Each one must give as he has decided in his heart, not reluctantly or under compulsion, for God loves a cheerful giver. And God is able to make all grace abound to you, so that having all sufficiency in all things at all times, you may abound in every good work" (2 Corinthians 9:7–8).

Trust that God knows your future. The 1 Chronicles 29:10–19 prayer of David is a great example for our prayer lives. But it is not until David gets to verse 18 that he actually petitions the Lord for anything. Up to this point, his prayer has consisted of praise, confession, and affirmation. Now David closes the prayer with specific requests:

> O Lord, the God of Abraham, Isaac, and Israel, our fathers, keep forever such purposes and thoughts in the hearts of your people, and direct their hearts toward you. Grant to Solomon my son a

whole heart that he may keep your commandments, your testimonies, and your statutes, performing all, and that he may build the palace for which I have made provision. (1 Chronicles 29:18–19)

In these final verses of David's prayer, he prays for the future of Israel. But David does not make a lot of prayer requests for the political, economic, military, physical, or geographic issues that Israel would surely have to face. He simply prays that the godly attitude they had demonstrated in their generous offering would continue in the days to come. He prays that God would keep their hearts set on Him. And he prays for Solomon, his son and successor, that God would give him wholehearted obedience to the will and word of God.

> **David prays for the future of Israel . . . not for the political, economic, military, issues but that God would keep their hearts set on him.**

As David is about to move off the scene, he prays for the future generation. And the major concern of his prayer requests is that God will keep their hearts right and obedient. David trusts the future into God's hands, confident that if the people's hearts are right, God will take care of them. Note that he does not leave that to chance. He prays that God would keep their hearts and make their hearts fully obedient.

You can have the same confidence today: If you take care of God's business, God will take care of your business. I believe that with all my heart. If you give yourself to God, God will take care of you. Look at these promises from God's Word:

Trust in the Lord with all your heart, and do not lean on your own understanding. In all your ways acknowledge him, and he will make straight your paths. (Proverbs 3:5–6)

But they who wait for the Lord shall renew their strength; they shall mount up with wings like eagles; they shall run and not be weary; they shall walk and not faint. (Isaiah 40:31)

But seek first the kingdom of God and his righteousness, and all these things will be added to you. (Matthew 6:33)

Give yourself to God, and watch God take care of you.

CHAPTER 8

God's Answer for Your
Anxiety

Do not be anxious about anything,
but in everything by prayer and supplication with thanksgiving
let your requests be made known to God.

PHILIPPIANS 4:6

Images of soldiers in battle are common in several of Paul's
epistles. That's not too surprising, considering he and his fellow
believers were all under rule by representatives of the Roman
Empire, which had conquered its territories with a mighty army.

Thus we're not surprised when Paul exhorts the church at
Philippi to "stand firm . . . in the Lord" (Philippians 4:1). The
picture is that of soldiers standing their ground in the face of opposition. We are to be courageous soldiers on the battlefield, not
frightened soldiers hiding in the barracks.

Philippians 4:1–9 is a call to Christian steadfastness. It is not the Lord's will that His people be wishy-washy. Christians should be strong, secure, and steadfast. Verses 2–8 teach practical steps that lead to the steadfastness of faith. And in the midst of these strategies Paul announces an essential part of this inspired strategies for Christian stability, one rooted in prayer: "Do not be anxious about anything, but in everything by prayer and supplication with thanksgiving let your requests be made known to God. And the peace of God, which surpasses all understanding, will guard your hearts and your minds in Christ Jesus" (verses 6–7).

BRING YOUR WORRIES TO GOD

The text begins with a command: "Do not be anxious about anything." The word *anxious* translates from a Greek verb that means to deeply care about something or someone. It can refer to proper or legitimate concern. Paul uses it this way when he says of his spiritual protégé, Timothy, "I have no one like him, who will be genuinely concerned for your welfare" (Philippians 2:20). But the word can also refer to sinful or undue concern. Jesus used the term this way when He said, "Martha, Martha, you are anxious and troubled about many things" (Luke 10:41).

Philippians 4:6 uses the term in this latter sense. Paul is not saying that we should be carefree or unconcerned about the important things, issues, and people in our lives. He is saying that we should not worry about them. Legitimate concern turns into sinful anxiety when we allow our hearts and minds to be pulled into different directions by our circumstances. Faith pulls us in one direction. Doubt pulls us in another direction. Similarly, hope pulls us in one direction; fear pulls us the opposite direction. And we find ourselves pulled apart with worry.

The word *worry* is derived from an Old English word that means *to strangle*. Yes, worry is internal strangulation. Jesus affirms this in the parable of the sower when He speaks of seed being planted among thorns: "This is the one who hears the word, but the cares of the world and the deceitfulness of riches choke the word, and it proves unfruitful" (Matthew 13:22).

So the apostle Paul wisely instructs the saints of God, "Do not be anxious about anything." The grammar of this command indicates that sinful anxiety was a present reality, not a potential threat. God is not just saying here, "Do not worry." He is saying, "Stop your worrying." God commands you and me to stop worrying. What are you worrying about? Is it your family? Is it your health? Is it your finances? Is it your job? Is it your future? Whatever it is, God says to stop worrying. But the Lord does not leave us there, with just a command to obey. God has given us an answer for your anxiety. He has shown us how to win over our worries.

> **God has shown us how to win over our worries. Here it is: Pray your worries away! Don't worry. Pray.**

Here it is: Pray your worries away!

Don't worry. Pray.

Turn your worries into prayers.

Take everything off of your worry list and put it on your prayer list.

Whenever you start to worry, stop and pray. Give each worry—one by one—to God in prayer.

In a real sense, every follower of the Lord Jesus Christ should let God do the worrying. The apostle Peter instructs each of us to be "casting all your anxieties on him, because he cares for you" (1 Peter 5:7).

Have you ever thought about that? God is worried about you! He's worried about your sin—that's why He sent His Son, Jesus Christ, to die on the cross.

God is intimately aware of what you're dealing with. He cares about your situation. And He is at work on your behalf.

He's worried about your sickness—that's why He has declared himself to be "Jehovah-Rapha," the God who heals.

He's worried about the daily affairs of your life—that's why He's the Good Shepherd who leads us in the paths of righteousness for His name's sake.

He's worried about your spiritual growth—that's why He has given the Holy Spirit and Scripture to facilitate your development in Christlikeness.

He's worried about your future—that's why He announced that He is the Alpha and Omega, the beginning and the end.

God is worried about you. Of course, God doesn't worry as we do—pacing the floor, scratching His head, and biting His fingernails. God is sovereign, holy, omniscient, omnipotent, and omnipresent. So God cannot have panic attacks. But He is worried about you in the sense that He is intimately aware of what you're dealing with. He cares about your situation. And He is actively at work on your behalf. The prophet Jeremiah declared, "For I know the plans I have for you, declares the Lord, plans for wholeness and not for evil, to give you a future and a hope" (Jeremiah 29:11). Do you believe that? If so, then what are you worrying about? Pray your troubles away.

How can you pray your troubles away?

REMEMBER THE PRIVILEGE OF PRAYER

Philippians 4:6 says, "Do not be anxious about anything, but in everything by prayer and supplication with thanksgiving let your requests be made known to God." This verse succinctly states the privilege of prayer with two words: "in everything."

Feel the tension of the text. Stop worrying. Start praying. Don't worry about anything. Pray about everything. Nothing is worth worrying about. Everything is worth praying about.

Did you get that? Worry and prayer cannot coexist. Worry and prayer are two great opposing forces, like fire and water, truth and error, light and darkness. So this verse teaches us that the way to be anxious for nothing is to be prayerful in everything.

And I want you to know that the word "everything" really means everything. There's no fine print, qualifiers, loopholes, or exceptions. We are to come to God about everything. Hebrews 4:16 says, "Let us then with confidence draw near to the throne of grace, that we may receive mercy and find grace to help in time of need." God has an open-door policy with those who trust Jesus Christ as their Savior and Lord. You don't have to be afraid. And you don't have to keep your worries to yourself. Our heavenly Father is interested in every detail of our lives. He has flung wide the gates to His presence and says, "Come and tell me all about it."

There is nothing too big for God to handle. A woman once asked G. Campbell Morgan, "Dr. Morgan, do you think we should pray about the little things in our lives?" He answered, "Madam, can you mention anything in our life that is big to God?"

He was right. Whatever it is, God can handle it. As John Newton wrote of our mighty King:

> Thou art coming to a king
> Large petitions with thee bring
> For his grace and power are such
> None can ever ask too much.[1]

Let me give you a single formula to make sense of life's problems. If you have a big God you have only little problems. But if you have a little God you have big problems. You should pray with confidence that God is a big God who can handle any situation.

Whatever is going on in your life, God can handle it. Jeremiah says, "Ah, Lord God! It is you who have made the heavens and the earth by your great power and by your outstretched arm! Nothing is too hard for you" (32:17). And God responded to the prophet's prayer with a rhetorical question to affirm Jeremiah's prayer: "Behold, I am the Lord, the God of all flesh. Is anything too hard for me?" (32:27). In the gospel of Luke, both an angel and Jesus affirm that truth: "For nothing will be impossible with God. . . . What is impossible with man is possible with God" (Luke 1:37; 18:27). There is nothing too big for God to handle.

There is nothing too small for God to care about. The Lord is actively involved in the monumental decisions, problems, and issues of our lives. The Lord also gets down into the nuts and bolts of life. God is the one who flung the sun, moon, and stars out into space. He is also the one who has numbered the hairs on your head. He is also the one who monitors the falling of every two-bit sparrow (see Matthew 6:26). The God who parted the waters in creation is also the one who turned water into wine for a newlywed couple who didn't order enough wine for the wedding reception. There is nothing too small for God to care about.

> **The God who flung the sun, moon, and stars out into space also has numbered the hairs on your head.**

God cares about the things that embarrass you.

God cares about your appliances that keep breaking down.

God cares about those lost keys that made you late.

God cares about those extra few minutes of sleep you need in the morning.

God cares about the things that you think are too silly to share with anybody else.

Let me bottom-line this for you: Whatever is going on in your life, if it matters to you, it matters to God.

REHEARSE THE PRACTICE OF PRAYER

A soldier was court-martialed after his superiors found him apparently sleeping on his post. His defense was that he was not asleep. He was praying. Of course, the authorities didn't buy that story. He was in trouble.

The prosecutor mocked the young soldier during the hearing. "Since you are such a praying person," he said, "offer a prayer for us now." Muffled giggling could be heard. But the soldier took this challenge seriously. Then right in the midst of the entire court, the young man offered a sincere, devout, and passionate prayer to God. When he finished, charges were dropped. The military tribunal concluded that he never would have been able to pray like that under pressure if he hadn't been practicing that kind of prayer before the pressure.[2]

Indeed, prayer is a privilege. But it is also a discipline. You must take the time and trouble to learn how to pray. If you are going to be able to pray your worries away, you must learn how to practice the discipline of prayer before problems arise, pressures attack, and pain afflicts you. What does it mean to practice the discipline of prayer?

> **Pray in order to spend time in personal, deliberate, and intimate communion with God— not just to get God to do something for you.**

Disciplined prayer involves time with God. The word "prayer" in Philippians 4:6 is from a Greek noun that is the broad, generic, all-encompassing word for prayer in the New Testament. It speaks of the act of addressing God. It is conversation and communion with God. It is the prayer that enjoys the presence of God and honors Him in worship. Paul uses it here to teach us that believing prayer involves time with God. When Paul writes in verse 6, "By prayer . . . let your requests be known to God," he is making the point that prayer should involve more than making requests to God. Your prayers should be more than the presentation of your sanctified wish list. You should pray in order to spend time in personal, deliberate, and intimate communion with

God—not just to get God to do something for you.

Daniel's enemies were jealous of his promotion. So they plotted against him. But they soon found out that Daniel could not be bribed, tempted, or discredited. He was too devoted to God. So they determined that if they couldn't get Daniel to break his devotion to God, they would set him up based on his devotion to God. They convinced King Darius to sign a decree prohibiting his subjects from praying for thirty days "to any God or man . . . except [the king]" (Daniel 6:7). The Bible says, "When Daniel knew that the document had been signed, he went to his house where he had windows in his upper chamber open toward Jerusalem. He got down on his knees three times a day and prayed and gave thanks before his God, as he had done previously" (v. 10).

Don't miss that last line. Daniel prayed, as was his custom. He prayed, as was his habit. He prayed, as was his practice. Daniel did not start praying when he heard the decree was signed. He was already praying. So when he received news that his enemies were plotting against him, he didn't worry about it. And he didn't panic to find out what to do next. Daniel just kept doing what he had already been doing. He prayed!

That may be why your prayers don't work. Many of us are practical atheists. We don't formally deny the existence of God. But we live as if He doesn't exist. We forget God when life gets good. Our prayers become perfunctory. Sometimes our church attendance becomes sporadic. For some of us, our giving becomes a tip rather than a tithe. Our service becomes inconsistent. And our time in the Word becomes nonexistent.

Then, when our money gets funny, our body gets sick, or our loved-ones start tripping, we rush to God for strength, guidance, and comfort.

I don't know about you, but I don't want to practice a crisis Christianity. It doesn't work. Paul said, "Do not be deceived: God is not mocked, for whatever one sows, that will he also reap" (Galatians 6:7). Listen, friend, you cannot plant wicked seeds and then quickly turn to God when you see that your harvest did not turn out the way you thought it would.

I am not saying that God cannot hear emergency prayers. I am saying that prayer without devotion to God is presumption. I cannot assert this strong enough. Prayer is like dialing 9-1-1. You try that and you may get put on hold like 9-1-1!

In contrast, true prayer is like two lovers getting together. They really don't have to go anywhere special; they just want to be together. And they don't have to have anything special to talk about. But they stay on the phone because neither one of them wants to hang up. Prayer should be like that. Authentic prayer involves time with God.

Disciplined prayer involves trust in God. Again, Philippians 4:6 says, "Do not be anxious about anything, but in everything by prayer and supplication with thanksgiving let your requests be made known to God." The word "supplication" refers to the act of entreaty or asking. The picture is that of an inferior bringing a petition to a superior. It is to pray with a sense of need. But supplication is not just about the act of taking your needs to God in prayer. It's about the spiritual implications of that act.

By taking your need to God in prayer, you are not informing God of something He does not know. Praise God for this next sentence: There are no breaking news flashes in heaven! God is omniscient. God knows everything known, unknown, and knowable. You cannot inform God of anything. By taking your needs to God in prayer, you are not telling Him something He does not know. You are affirming that God is the one who is able to meet your need.

> **In prayer, you are not informing God of something He does not know. You are affirming that God is the one who is able to meet your need.**

Supplication is a statement of trust in God. It is a declaration of dependence upon God. It's the simple act of confessing to God that you are going to trust God with your situation. Jesus taught this in Matthew 6:25–34. It is the section of the Sermon on the Mount where Jesus directly addresses the issue of worry. His position on worry is clear and simple: Don't do it. Don't worry about what you will eat or drink or wear. And don't worry about tomorrow. Gerald Mann suggests that Jesus does not tell us not to worry, as much as He tells us to wait to worry. Mann notes that Jesus gives us only four times when we may begin to worry:

Worry when it will feed and clothe you.

Worry when it will make you live longer or grow taller.

Worry when you want to know how people who don't worry react to problems.

Worry when you want to make tomorrow worse than it's already going to be.[3]

Wait to worry until then. In the meantime, Jesus says, "But

seek first the kingdom of God and his righteousness, and all these things will be added to you" (Matthew 6:33). That's God's affirmative action program. That's God's stimulus program. That's God's guaranteed insurance policy. Mark it down: Worry is like sitting in a rocking chair—it gives you something to do, but it doesn't get you anywhere. So trust God no matter what. Put God first in everything. Expect God to come alongside of you and place what you need before you.

Authentic prayer involves thanksgiving to God. One reason many of us worry so much is because we are ungrateful people. We

> **I dare you to make thanksgiving a habit. Your doubts would dissolve. Your fears would subside.**

don't thank God enough. And because we are often short on praise, we are short on peace. If the Lord was stingy, close-handed, and inconsistent in blessing us, we would be more grateful for every single thing He did. However, we respond to God's extravagant grace with indifference. Consequently, we spend more time rehearsing what's not going right in our lives, rather than rejoicing over the undeserved goodness of God. But I dare you to make thanksgiving a habit. Your worries would vanish. Your doubts would dissolve. Your fears would subside.

Philippians 4:6 instructs us to make our requests to God "with thanksgiving." This does not mean that when your prayers are finally answered; you should go back and thank God. On the contrary, the phrase "with thanksgiving" means that gratitude is to characterize the very act of prayer—not just the answer to it. When you make your requests—right then and there—thank God.

Psalm 100:4 says, "Enter his gates with thanksgiving, and his courts with praise! Give thanks to him; bless his name!" If we obeyed this verse, it would revolutionize our worship. Too often we drag into worship discouraged and even defeated. We wait for something to happen in the service to get us in the mood to worship. But that is not how it should be. You should enter into his gates with thanksgiving. You should enter into his courts with praise. You should not need musicians, choirs, worship leaders, deacons, or preachers to get you into the mood to worship God. You should have a praise on the inside for all that the Lord has done for you through Jesus Christ. Hymn writer Johnson Oatman Jr. captures this attitude in his hymn "Count Your Blessings":

> When upon life's billows you are tempest tossed,
> When you are discouraged, thinking all is lost,
> Count your many blessings, name them one by one,
> And it will surprise you what the Lord hath done.[4]

RECEIVE THE PROMISE OF PRAYER

I have good news and bad news for you. When you go to God in believing prayer, you can expect God to respond to your prayer. God hears. God knows. God cares. God answers. God responds when you pray. That's the good news. The bad news is that He may not respond the way you want him to.

After telling believers to pray (Philippians 4:6), the apostle Paul adds, "And the peace of God, which surpasses all understanding, will guard your hearts and minds in Christ Jesus" (v. 7). This wonderful promise affirms that God will respond when you pray. But it does not promise that God will change your circumstances. No healings. No new job. No deliverance. No supernatural debt cancellation. No promotion. No Mr. or Miss Right. No miracles. The verse does not promise divine intervention for your circumstances. But it does promise divine insulation for your heart and mind. *The promise of prayer is peace.*

This is not to say that God is unable or unwilling to move in your circumstances. He is. But that's not the point here. The point is that God is more concerned about what's within you than He is about what's going on around you. God is more concerned about what's happening in you than He is what's happening to you.

Have things really changed, as a result of your prayers? Not necessarily. You may still be in a war zone. The battle may still be raging. The enemy may still be advancing. But even though war is raging around you, something has happened within you. God has dispatched His peace to guard your heart and mind. That's the promise of the text.

In fact, that's God's promise throughout Scripture. Isaiah 26:3 says, "You keep him in perfect peace whose mind is stayed on you, because he trusts in you." Colossians 3:15 says, "And let the peace of Christ rule in your hearts, to which indeed you were called in one body. And be thankful." And Jesus Himself says, "Peace I leave with you; my peace I give to you. Not as the world gives do I give to you. Let not your hearts be troubled, neither let them be afraid" (John 14:27).

God will give you peace that "surpasses all understanding."

People in your life who know what you are going through won't be able to understand how you are calm, joyful, and at peace. And you won't be able to explain it. "All understanding" means you can't understand it either. You don't know how you have so much peace in the midst of so much confusion. Let me explain: It's the peace of God!

As we noted, although King Darius had issued a decree prohibiting his subjects from praying to anyone but him for thirty days, that did not stop Daniel from continuing to pray to the true God. For this act of devotion Daniel received the death penalty. Darius put him in a lion's den and put a stone on the mouth of the den, so he couldn't escape.

What happened next is revealing. "Then the king went to his palace and spent the night fasting; no diversions were brought to him, and sleep fled from him" (Daniel 6:18). He was in the palace, but he couldn't sleep. Surrounded by luxuries, and protected by armed soldiers and trained guards, the king couldn't sleep. He stayed up all night long.

The next morning he rushed down to the lions' den and called out to Daniel. To his surprise, Daniel answered. "My God sent his angel and shut the lions' mouths" (v. 22). The king couldn't sleep all night, yet God was keeping the lions quiet so that His child Daniel could rest in safety. That's what the peace of God will do for you, if you take your worries to God in prayer.

A ship was wrecked in a furious storm and the only survivor was a little boy who was swept by the waves onto a rock. He sat there all night long, until he was spotted and rescued the next morning. "Did you tremble while you were on the rock during the night?" someone asked. "Yes," said the boy. "I trembled all night. But the rock didn't move." That's the testimony of every Christian who subscribes to God's answer for anxiety.

CHAPTER 9

Praying with Spiritual
Priorities

And so, from the day we heard, we have not ceased to pray for you,
asking that you may be filled with the knowledge of
his will in all spiritual wisdom and understanding.

COLOSSIANS 1:9

One of the most helpful things you can do to strengthen your
prayer life is to study the prayers of the apostle Paul as
recorded in the New Testament. Most of Paul's letters begin with
a thanksgiving and prayer for "the saints" (believers) to whom he
writes. Paul does not simply tell the saints that he is praying for
them. Moved by the Spirit, Paul reports the content of his prayers.
These prayer reports are lessons in how to pray.

One of those exemplary prayers of Paul appears in Colossians
1:9–14. The apostle has already told the church that he regularly
prays for them (v. 3). Now he tells them exactly what he prays on

their behalf. But this is more than a glimpse into the private prayer life of the great apostle. It is the God-breathed Scripture that is profitable for teaching and training us in prayer.

Paul's prayer for the Colossians is a model of intercession. It shows us how spiritual leaders should pray for those under their care. At the same time, it shows us members of the church how we should pray for our leaders and for one another, as brothers and sisters in Christ. It also shows us how to bring our own needs and concerns and burdens to the Lord in prayer.

In this chapter, I want to focus on the main prayer requests Paul makes for the Colossians. But there is a lesson in Paul's example of prayer before you get to his petitions. First of all, it is noteworthy that we find Paul in prayer. The epistle to the Colossians is one of the Prison Epistles of Paul. He did not write this letter while on sabbatical or in a secluded pastor's study. Paul was under house arrest in Rome, where he was awaiting trial. He did not know whether he would be convicted and executed or vindicated and released. In the meantime, there he was, imprisoned, chained to Roman soldiers.

Yet Paul was not in prison blaming God or pitying himself or complaining to others. Paul prayed.

What about you? When you face troubles, pressures, and uncertainties, how do you respond? Do you worry? Do you complain? Or do you pray? For the sake of argument, let's assume you pray. But if you were in Paul's predicament, what would you pray? Most of us would pray for the obvious. We would pray for God to get us out of jail. Or for a good lawyer. Or for protection from the various dangers of imprisonment. But as you read through this prayer, you'll see that Paul's requests were not preoccupied with the difficult situation he found himself in. He prayed for the Colossians. Paul prayed for others, not just himself.

Paul was moved to pray for the Colossians after the report he received from Epaphras about the condition of the church. For the most part, it was good news for which Paul gave thanks to God (vv. 3–8). Yet Paul still prayed for the Colossians after receiving this good report. This is instructive. All too often, we pray for others only after receiving bad news of personal sin, health concerns, family crises, financial reversals, and other difficult circumstances. We intercede for those who are doing poorly and ignore those who are doing well. We are quick to pray for those who are obviously weak but are often slow to pray for those who are apparently strong. But Paul was wise enough to know that there were dangers, toils, and snares down the road. So he prayed for these saints after receiving a good report about them.

And Paul did not just pray for them once or twice in passing. Paul prayed for the Colossians unceasingly. This is an essential mark of effective prayer. It is diligent, persistent, and continual. That is how Paul prayed for the Colossians—unceasingly. This is all the more remarkable when you consider that Paul and the Colossians had never met face-to-face. Theirs was a relationship of correspondence. Paul had not visited this church. Yet Paul continually prayed for them. Ouch. There are many times we fail to pray for our closest family and friends. But Paul prayed unceasingly for people he had never even met.

How do you pray for someone you have never met—when you

do not know the person or the circumstances? How do you pray when you don't know what to pray? You know you need to pray. You may even want to pray. But you do not know what to pray.

I believe Colossians 1:9–14 is the answer. As we read through this prayer, it's obvious that Paul does not pray about physical or material or even relational circumstances of the Colossians. Of course, this is not to say that you should not pray about your health, finances, family, career, or goals. You ought to pray about everything. But when something is not right in a believer's life, or in a local church, the heart of the matter is always the matter of the heart. We are prone to focus on our circumstances. But God focuses on our hearts.

Many times we fail to pray for our closest family and friends. But Paul prayed unceasingly for people he had never even met.

As Proverbs 4:23 tells us, "Keep your heart with all vigilance, for from it flow the springs of life."

God is always more concerned about what is happening in you than He is about what is happening to you.

God is always more concerned about what is happening within you than He is about what is happening around you.

God is always more concerned about your internal disposition than He is about your external situation.

So Paul prayed about heart-level issues. He prayed for needs, issues, and concerns that were underneath the skin. He prayed about spiritual priorities. In so doing, Paul shows us how we should pray when we don't know what to pray.

PRAY FOR DEVOTION TO GOD'S WILL

The request. The apostle reports, "And so, from the day we heard, we have not ceased to pray for you, asking that you may be filled with the knowledge of his will in all spiritual wisdom and understanding" (Colossians 1:9). What is Paul asking God for here? Well, let's determine that by clarifying what he is not asking.

First of all, Paul does not pray for God to place the Colossians in His divine will. He assumed the circumstances these saints faced were not accidental or incidental. Paul took it for granted that the Lord had a plan and purpose for the Colossians. The same is true of you and your situation. As God's child, there are no accidents in your life! You can live with the assurance that the invisible hand of providence is busy at work on your situation. Right now. "For I know the plans I have for you, declares the Lord, plans for welfare and not for evil, to give you a future and a hope" (Jeremiah 29:11). The Lord has a good purpose for your life (Romans 8:29). And He is sure to bring it to pass (Philippians 1:6).

Likewise, Paul does not ask God to reveal His will to the Colossians. He prayed with assurance that God had a plan for their lives and that God wanted them to know His plan that they may walk in it. In another letter written from a Roman jail, Paul instructs, "Look carefully then how you walk, not as unwise but as wise, making the best use of the time, because the days are evil. Therefore do not be foolish, but understand what the will of the Lord is" (Ephesians 5:15–17). God does not play hide-and-go-seek when it comes to the revelation of His will. God has a plan for your life. And God wants you to know His will so that you may walk in His will.

Well, how can we discern God's will for our lives? Paul answers, "And so, from the day we heard, we have not ceased to pray for you, asking that you may be filled with the knowledge of his will in all spiritual wisdom and understanding" (Colossians 1:9). God's will is revealed through spiritual wisdom and understanding.

I was a very young man when I began my first pastoral assignment. And I was naïve. I thought that if you just taught the church what the Bible says, members would fall in line with the truth. Very naïve. I was dragged into the real world by members who said, "Now, wait a minute, Junior. We're saved. And we believe the Bible. But God also gave us common sense." Admittedly, I did not know how to respond to this initially. What was I going to say? I couldn't disagree. I was not going to say, "You're wrong. God didn't give you common sense!" I had to agree that God gives common sense. But that is not the whole story. While God gives common sense, the Bible never instructs us to seek spiritual discernment through common sense. There are some things the Lord is up to in your life that cannot be figured out through common sense. And there are some things the Lord is doing in His church that cannot be understood through mere common sense. You need spiritual wisdom and understanding.

Consider Solomon's wise instruction to his son: "Trust in the Lord with all your heart, and do not lean on your own understanding" (Proverbs 3:5). In other words, trust God. Do not trust what you think you know. Your understanding is not strong or stable enough for you to lean on. Solomon added, "In all your ways acknowledge him, and he will make straight your paths" (Proverbs 3:6).

What, then, is Paul asking for when he prays "that you may be filled with the knowledge of his will in all spiritual wisdom and understanding" (Colossians 1:9)? I believe the key to this prayer is found in the word "filled." It means to bring something to its saturation point, or level of containment. It simply means to be filled. But when the word is used metaphorically, as it is here, it denotes totality. The idea is that something that is already full does not have room for anything else. So when Scripture speaks of being filled with something, it means that thing is the driving force, controlling presence, or dominating presence in our lives. For instance, Paul exhorts the Ephesian saints, "Be filled with the Spirit" (Ephesians 5:18). That is, they were to submit to the governing influence of the Holy Spirit in their lives. In the same way, Paul prays that the believers of Colossae would be filled with, governed by, and submissive to the will of God in their lives.

> **Paul prays that the believers of Colossae would be filled with, governed by, and submissive to the will of God.**

Could this be the reason why you struggle to discern God's will for your life? You may be unable to discern God's will because you are unwilling to devote to God's will. You can't know it if you won't do it. We should pray like trusting children going to a heavenly Father for spiritual wisdom. But we often pray like shrewd businessmen doing cutthroat negotiations in a corporate boardroom. We have a need. And we present it to God in prayer. Then we wait for God to make His best offer. We consider God's bid. But we don't sign the deal too quickly. We want to keep our options open, just in case God is not saying what we want to hear. But you cannot discern God's will for your life that way. God does not reveal His will for entertainment purposes only. God reveals His will to those who have a precommitment to obey.

As Jesus taught in the temple, the people were amazed. They wanted to know how Jesus had such depth of understanding, seeing that He had not been to rabbinical school. How could he understand theology so well having never been to seminary? Jesus answered, "If anyone's will is to do God's will, he will know whether the teaching is from God or whether I am speaking on my own authority" (John 7:17). Jesus would not satisfy their curiosity. The truth about Him would only be revealed to those who desire to do God's will. You cannot know the will of God if you do not will to do His will. To discern God's will, you must devote yourself to God's will. You must be able to say, "If it's God's will, I will."

The reason. Why does Paul pray that the saints be filled with the knowledge of God's will? As he explains: "so as to walk in a manner worthy of the Lord" (v. 10). When Paul speaks of how we "walk," he is talking about more than putting one foot after another to get from one place to another. To "walk," metaphorically, involves movement, progress, and consistency. It is about your lifestyle, consistent conduct, or habitual behavior. It is about how you live your life.

This is why Paul prays that the Colossians be filled with the knowledge of God's will. It is necessary for us to walk in a manner that is worthy of the Lord. The word translated "worthy" means to be comparable to a standard. The word originally referred to scales. Then it was used for what is placed on a scale. It later developed to refer to one thing being comparable to another, as if on a scale. Paul uses this interesting word in prayer, asking the Lord to help the church to live up to God's standards for their lives.

> **Lincoln: "The real question is not whether God is on our side, but whether we are on God's side."**

In praying this way, Paul makes it clear that God does not exist to fulfill our expectations of Him. God does not do our bidding. He is not our servant. We exist to fulfill God's expectations of us. We are to live up to God's standards. We are to walk in a manner that is worthy of the Lord.

During the United States Civil War, President Abraham Lincoln was asked if he thought God was on the side of the Union, rather than with the cause of the Confederates. Lincoln responded, "The real question is not whether God is on our side, but whether we are on God's side." Lincoln was right. What matters the most is that we are on God's side. We must walk in a manner worthy of the Lord. You should do what God is blessing rather than trying to get God to bless what you are doing.

The result. How can I know whether I am walking in a manner worthy of the Lord? Paul explains in the second half of verse 10: "so as to walk in a manner worthy of the Lord, fully pleasing to him, bearing fruit in every good work and increasing in the knowledge of God."

Note the progression of this prayer. Paul prays that the church would be filled with the knowledge of God's will in order to walk worthy of the Lord. Then he says the first sign that you are walking right is that you are more concerned about pleasing God than you are about pleasing people—you will be "fully pleasing to him." What does it mean to be fully pleasing to the Lord? The Greek term Paul uses here to speak of pleasing the Lord once referred to one who would do anything to please someone else, be it illegal, immoral, or unethical. Paul slips this term into the lexicon of the church to say that you should *not* be willing to do whatever it takes to please people. But you should be willing to do whatever it takes to please the Lord. We should be "fully pleasing" to the Lord. We should not be content to merely get a passing grade, sliding by with a C–. We should strive to get 100 percent on every assignment God gives us.

It is easy to fall in the trap of trying to please people. One day, a father and his son walked their mule to the marketplace. As they walked alongside the mule, they passed a group of people who criticized them for walking instead of riding the mule. So the father got on and the son walked. Then they passed another group of people who criticized the father for riding while making his son walk. Hearing these complaints, the father got off the mule and the son got on. Then they passed another group of people who criticized the son for being so disrespectful, riding in comfort and making his father walk. So they both got on the mule. Then they passed another group of people who criticized them for working that poor mule so hard. The point of the story is that if you live to please people, you will either lose your mule or lose your mind!

Remember the warning of Proverbs 29:25: "The fear of man lays a snare, but whoever trusts in the Lord is safe."

The second way to please God—which shows that you are living according to God's will—is to be "bearing fruit in every good work." The New Testament is emphatic that no one can be saved by performing good works. God is holy and we are not. And our biggest problem is that we will have to answer to God for how we have lived our lives. All of us have sinned and fall short of the glory of God (Romans 3:23). Worse, we can do nothing to win the approval of God. We are guilty sinners who fall woefully short of God's righteous standards. How then can sinners get right with God?

> **Although we are not saved *by* good works, we are saved *for* good works.**

Ephesians 2:8–9 answers, "For by grace you have been saved through faith. And this is not your own doing; it is the gift of God, not a result of works, so that no one may boast." Note what this passage teaches us about the way of salvation. We are saved by grace. We are saved through faith. And we are saved for good works. As Paul notes, "We are his workmanship, created in Christ Jesus for good works, which God prepared beforehand, that we should walk in them" (v. 10).

Although we are not saved *by* good works, we are saved *for* good works. God has so ordered our lives that we would fulfill the good works He has preordained for us to do. In his prayer for the Philippians, Paul asks that they be "filled with the fruit of righteousness that comes through Jesus Christ, to the glory and praise of God."

Finally, living according to God's will means we will please God by "increasing in the knowledge of God." Paul reveals to the Philippian church the consuming passion of his life: "that I may know

him and the power of his resurrection, and may share his suffer-
ings, becoming like him in his death" (Philippians 3:10). When he
writes of this desire, Paul has been walking with the Lord for thirty
years! He knows the Lord. He has introduced many people to the
Lord. He's planted churches, written letters, and mentored leaders
to spread the knowledge of the Lord. It can be argued that no human
being knew the Lord better than Paul. What does he mean by writing, "that I may know him"?

Paul wants to know the Lord better. He wants to know Him
more deeply, personally, and intimately. And Paul's desire is the divine mandate for every follower of Christ. The apostle Peter adds,
"But grow in the grace and knowledge of our Lord and Savior
Jesus Christ" (2 Peter 3:18).

PRAY WITH DEPENDENCE UPON GOD'S POWER

The request. Paul prays, "May you be strengthened with all
power, according to his glorious might, for all endurance and patience with joy" (Colossians 1:11). This prayer request emphasizes
how vital it is that we live in dependence upon God's power.

First of all, the power of God is necessary. Paul does not stop
his prayer after asking that the saints be filled with the knowledge
of God's will. He also prays that they be strengthened with all
power. Both are necessary to walk in the will of God for your life.
Sure, you need God's help to be submissive to His will. But you also
need divine help to obey the will of God. You cannot do God's will
in your strength. Jesus says, "I am the vine; you are the branches.
Whoever abides in me and I in him, he it is that bears much fruit,

for apart from me you can do nothing" (John 15:5). This is the key to a fruitful life. You must acknowledge that God the Father is the gardener (15:1–2). You must embrace the Lord Jesus Christ as the True Vine. And you must remember that you are just a branch.

Likewise, the power of God is available. This prayer request provides simple, practical, and helpful advice for the burdens you carry, as well as the opposition and challenges you face. Pray about it. And don't stop praying! If you pray about it, God will give you strength as strength is needed. "But they who wait for the Lord shall renew their strength," says Isaiah, "they shall mount up with wings like eagles; they shall run and not be weary; they shall walk and not faint" (40:31). God will give you strength as it is needed. He will give you strength to mount up over a sudden storm like an eagle. The promise is not that you will feel strong. You may feel anything but strong. If so, that's a good thing. The weaker you feel, the more you will lean on the Lord.

The apostle Paul is a witness to having God's strength when we feel weak. He was given "a thorn in the flesh" to keep him from being lifted up in pride. We do not know exactly what this thorn was. But whatever it was, it hurt. Paul took this painful situation to the Lord in prayer. Three times, he asked the Lord to take it away. The Lord refused (2 Corinthians 12:7–9). Don't miss that. It's a fact about prayer you can't afford to ignore. Sometimes, God says no. But there is always a yes imbedded within the no. The Lord did not answer Paul's prayer. But He answered the prayer Paul should have prayed. "My grace is sufficient for you," said the Lord, "for my power is made perfect in weakness" (v. 9).

Indeed, the power of God is sufficient. Paul prays, "May you be strengthened with all power, according to his glorious might" (Colossians 1:11). The phrase "according

> **The strength God provides is according to His exhaustive sovereignty, not your limited resources.**

to" is significant. It means that the strength God provides is according to His exhaustive sovereignty, not your limited resources. Sometimes we look at how great the challenge is and how limited our strength is and we conclude that we cannot prevail. We just glance at God, but we gaze at Goliath. Look again. If that is the conclusion you have drawn, you are looking in the wrong direction. The question is not whether you can do it. It is whether God can do it. I want you to know that God can do it for you!

Ask Joshua and Caleb. Moses sent out twelve spies into Canaan to see if the Lord was telling the truth about the Promised Land (Numbers 13). Upon their return, ten of the spies reported that every good thing God said was in the land was there. They even brought back evidence. But they had a bad report. There were giants in the land. "We should not go forward," they concluded. "We look like grasshoppers in their sight, and in our own sight" (paraphrase of Numbers 13:33). But there was another report. Caleb and Joshua also saw the giant people. But knowing their powerful God, Caleb said on behalf of Joshua, "We are well able to overcome [the land]" (13:30; see also 14:6–9). May the Lord give you ruthless trust in the face of overwhelming circumstances that concludes that nothing is impossible with God!

The reason. Why do we need to "be strengthened with all power according to his glorious might"? Paul's gives the reason in the second half of verse 11: "for all endurance and patience with joy."

Consider what Paul does not say. We do not need divine enablement in order to preach, teach, lead, witness, sing, or serve. You need divine enablement "for all endurance and patience with joy." "Endurance and patience" are parallel terms. But there is a subtle nuance that makes an important point. The word "endurance" is from a Greek word that means "to remain under." It is the word the New Testament uses to describe how Christians should respond to difficult circumstances. You are under a heavy load, but you do not quit. You keep going forward, even though you are carrying a heavy load. The word "patience" is better translated "longsuffering." It is the word the New Testament uses to describe how Christians should respond to difficult people. It means that you are slow to anger. You do not have a quick fuse. People do not easily push your buttons.

> **God does not want the saints to be weak, unstable, reactionary Christians. He wants you to have staying power.**

This is why you need divine enablement. In your Christian walk, there will be times when you will have to deal with difficult circumstances and crazy people. Paul prays this way because God does not want the saints to be weak, unstable, reactionary Christians who run from church to church, job to job, city to city, relationship to relationship, when things do not go their way. God wants us to have staying power. As followers of the risen Savior, we should be "steadfast, immovable, always abounding in the work of the Lord, knowing that in the Lord your labor is not in vain" (1 Corinthians 15:58).

When God gives you strength, it will not be grit-your-teeth, grin-and-bear it, "I'll do it if it kills me" endurance and patience. It will be endurance and patience with joy. You are going through a big challenge. And those who know what you are going through expect to see you with a broken heart, bowed head, and heavy spirit. But to their surprise you are full of joy. No, you are not happy about what you are going through. But you have joy in spite of what you are going through. James 1:2–3 says, "Count it all joy, my brothers, when you meet trials of various kinds, for you know that the testing of your faith produces steadfastness."

PRAY WITH THANKFULNESS

The results. What are the intended results of this prayer for divine enablement? How can you identify one who has been "strengthened with all power according to his glorious might"? What is the difference between a strong Christian and a weak Christian? Colossians 1:12 answers: "giving thanks to the Father." What a challenging thought. The distinctive mark of a strong Christian is that he or she gives thanks in all circumstances (1 Thessalonians 5:18). Strong Christians are grateful people.

Weak Christians can thank God only when the sun is shining.

Weak Christians can thank God only when things are going their way.

Weak Christians can thank God only when they have money in the bank.

Weak Christians can thank God only when their family is at peace.

Weak Christians can thank God only when their career is on track.

But strong Christians are perpetually thankful. The psalmist declares, "Enter his gates with thanksgiving, and his courts with praise! Give thanks to him; bless his name!" (Psalm 100:4). Is this how you come before the presence of God?

What do I have to thank God for? you may ask. Paul explains:

> giving thanks to the Father, who has qualified you to share in the inheritance of the saints in light. He has delivered us from the domain of darkness and transferred us to the kingdom of his beloved Son, in whom we have redemption, the forgiveness of sins. (Colossians 1:12–14)

In short, Paul says that we should thank God above all things for our salvation. If you've received Jesus Christ as your Savior and Lord by faith, you always have something to thank God for. And you don't have to check your bank account to find a reason to thank God. You don't have to live in a big house in a gated community to find a reason to thank God. You can thank God that you are saved!

What happens after you pray? A lot of things, including the ability to know God's will, be pleasing to God, and increase in your relationship with God. And it all starts with accepting God's salvation through the Lord Jesus. That's why we can be thankful to the Father, "who has qualified you to share in the inheritance of the saints" (v. 12).

So thank God that you are saved.

Thank God that He has qualified you to share in the inheritance of the saints in light.

Thank God that He has delivered you from the domain of darkness.

Thank God that He has transferred you into the kingdom of His beloved Son.

Thank God that He has redeemed you.

Thank God that He has forgiven your sins by the blood of Jesus.

Thank God that He hears and answers the prayers of those who belong to Him in Christ.

Conclusion

It was the longest Monday ever. I was a young pastor in the midst of congregational turmoil. A church meeting had been scheduled for that evening, and the formal agenda announced. But the meeting would be spent complaining about me.

Things had reached a boiling point, and I fully expected someone to make a move on me that night. Either I would be effectively marginalized or dismissed. There was no way this could turn out in my favor.

Three years earlier the church leaders had searched for a new pastor to take over for my father, who had pastored there four full decades. I was still a senior in high school. But the night the church met to call a new pastor, they selected me.

I had not made a mess of things. The church was actually growing. But many people now felt I was too young to pastor the church. Several of my opponents told me they were going to put me out, but assured me I was young enough to bounce back at some time.

I was at a crisis point. My father had led the church with a firm hand. But I was now taking the punches they could not land on him. No one was really speaking up for me. Supporters were slowly backing away. I felt alone. I fasted that day, but not on purpose. I couldn't eat.

I didn't want to talk to anyone. I just sat staring at the walls. In the quietness, I sensed the Lord telling me to pray. Honestly, that was the last thing I wanted to do. So I called a friend and asked for prayer. But as I listened to the prayer, I felt convicted. I was being disobedient. I needed to pray for myself.

It was a struggle, but I did it. For the rest of the afternoon, I wrestled with God in prayer. I didn't have the faith to ask Him to turn things in my favor. I was not sure I wanted Him to. But I finally decided that I would serve and praise the Lord no matter what happened.

They weight of my anxieties lifted. I felt all would be well, even though I had no clue what would happen next.

I learned that day that it happens after prayer. It does not happen after you read about prayer, talk about prayer, or hear a stirring message about prayer. It happens after prayer. Do you believe that? Do you believe God hears and answers prayer? The proof of faith is obedience. It is not about what you think or say. It is about what you do.

I hope this book has challenged you to a life of prayer. Trust the sovereignty, wisdom, and goodness of God. Don't stop praying. No, I cannot guarantee that prayer will bring the results you want in life. But prayer will align your heart with God's will. As you pray, God works. His ways are best. His plans are good. And His power is unlimited.

Notes

Chapter 1: It Happens after Prayer

1. See the commands of Jesus and the apostles Paul and James in Matthew 5:39, 41, 43–44; Luke 17:4; Romans 12:21; 1 Corinthians 15:58; 1 Thessalonians 5:18; James 1:2.

2. Frederick Buechner, *Wishful Thinking*, rev. ed. (San Francisco: Harper One, 1993), n.p.

3. Joseph Scriven, "What a Friend We Have in Jesus." In public domain.

Chapter 2: God Is Not a Sleepy Friend

1. William Barclay, *The Gospel of Luke*, 2nd ed. (Louisville: Westminster John Knox, 1975), 146.

Chapter 3: God Is Not a Crooked Judge

1. As quoted in Dan Graves, "Richard C. Trench Loved Words," www. christianity.com/church/church-history/timeline/1801-1900/richard-c-trench-loved-words-11630435.html. A writer of commentaries on several New Testament books, as well as a poet and philologist, Trench eventually became the bishop of Dublin.

Chapter 4: The Wise Prayer of a Weak Man

1. William Arnot, *Studies in Proverbs* (Grand Rapids: Kregel, 1998), 567.

2. R. J. Morgan, *Nelson's Complete Book of Stories, Illustrations, and Quotes* (Nashville: Nelson, 1952), 574.

3. Arnot, *Studies in Proverbs*.

4. This listing of God's blessings upon us are found in James 1:17; Acts 17:25, 28; Psalm 23:5; Ephesians 1:3; Philippians 4:9; 1 Timothy 6:17.

Chapter 5: The Kind of Prayer God Answers

1. Elisha A. Hoffman, "I Must Tell Jesus," 1893. In public domain.

2. Brennan Manning, *Abba's Child* (Colorado Springs: NavPress, 2002), 159.

3. Francis Thompson, "The Hound of Heaven, http://www.bartleby.com/236/239.html. Written in 1893, the poem appeared in the *Oxford Book of English Mystical Verse* in 1917.

Chapter 7: A Godly Attitude toward Material Possessions

1. Milo Kauffman, *Stewards of God* (Eugene, Oreg.: Wipf & Stock, 2001), 174.

Chapter 8: God's Answer for Your Anxiety

1. John Newton, "Untitled Hymn," *Olney Hymns* (London: W. Oliver, 1779). In public domain.

2. Paul L. Tan, *Encyclopedia of 7,700 Illustrations* (Thousand Oaks, Calif.: Assurance Books, 1979), 1040.

3. Gerard Mann, *Common Sense Religion* (Helena, Mont.: Riverbend, 1998), 135–36.

4. Johnson Oatman Jr., "Count Your Blessings." In public domain.

Acknowledgments

I am much taller than my short stature indicates, for I stand on the shoulders of many good and godly people. The publication of this book is another example of the ways the Lord has used others to help me along the way.

It has been a joy to partner on this book with the Moody Publishers team. Thanks to Karen Waddles for holding this door open for me. And special thanks to Roslyn Jordan, Donielle Alicea, and Jim Vincent for their partnership in preparing the manuscript for publication.

I am grateful for Ray Pritchard, who graciously consented to write the foreword for this work. His friendship, preaching, and writing have been an immeasurable benefit to me. And I am honored to have him commend this book.

I am indebted to the writers whose books have clarified my understanding of what the Bible teaches about prayer and have motivated me to pray.

The people of Mt. Sinai Church of Los Angeles always believed there was a writer in me. As a boy, this congregation introduced me to Jesus and instilled the priority of prayer within me. Later, for seventeen years, they nurtured me as I pastored them. Their love, prayers, and encouragement continue to undergird me. I thank my God at every remembrance of you (Phil. 1:3).

I am privileged to serve as the pastor-teacher of a wonderful congregation of saints at the Shiloh Metropolitan Baptist Church of Jacksonville. I am grateful for their prayers and support as I worked on this project. More specifically, I want to express my deep appreciation to the Shiloh pastors and staff, for their partnership in the gospel that enabled me to give myself to writing.

A special word of thanks goes to my executive assistant, Nicole Clark, for helping me to get this projecrt across the finish line.

My wife, Crystal, is my best friend, ministry partner, and greatest source of encouragement. She has constantly prodded me to write. Now that I have concluded this project, she is prodding me to write again! It is only because of the home she has made for our family that I am able to do anything productive. I married way out of my league! Thanks for everything you do. I love you.

Our children—H. B. III, Natalie, and Hailey—have cheered me on as I worked on this book. They deserve as much credit for this book as anyone else. You mean the world to me.

Ultimately, I praise the Lord Jesus Christ for His High Priestly ministry that gives me and all His followers access to the throne of grace (Hebrews 4:14–16). Through His blood and righteousness we enjoy the privilege of prayer and the blessed assurance that it happens after prayer!